CW00349367

CROSSING BOUNDARIES
WITH
THE COMMUNITY
FOREST PATH

1: Out From The Centre

Christopher Bloor

Closer To The Countryside

First published in 2007 by
Closer to the Countryside (Books)
161 Wellington Hill West,
Henleaze,
Bristol BS9 4QW

© Christopher Bloor

ISBN 978-0-9555461-0-5

Printed in the UK by Biddles of Norfolk

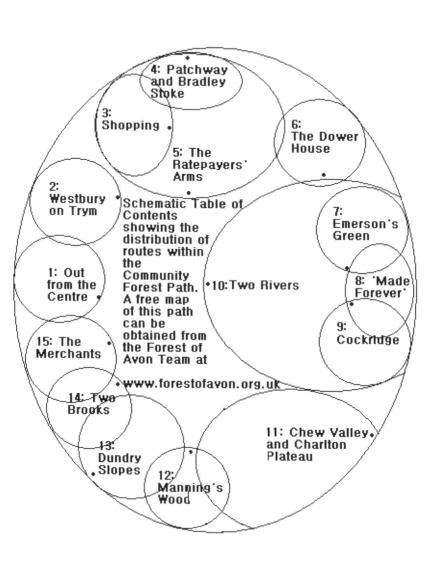

4: Patchway and Bradley Stoke

3: Shopping

5: The Ratepayers' Arms

6: The Dower House

2: Westbury on Trym

7: Emerson's Green

1: Out from the Centre

Schematic Table of Contents showing the distribution of routes within the Community Forest Path. A free map of this path can be obtained from the Forest of Avon Team at

10:Two Rivers

8: 'Made Forever'

9: Cockridge

15: The Merchants

www.forestofavon.org.uk

14: Two Brooks

11: Chew Valley and Charlton Plateau

13: Dundry Slopes

12: Manning's Wood

INTRODUCTION

For ten years, the Community Forest Path has girdled Bristol through some of the beautiful green spaces that make up the Forest of Avon. Unfortunately, although many sections of the path are well used, others remain 'untrodden ways'.

The path is a wonderful resource and deserves to be better known, and the aim of this book is to bring the path to a wider audience. Three factors conspire against this outcome. Firstly, on the whole, people do not live in green spaces. That is what makes them attractive. Secondly, the path crosses administrative boundaries, so few people have a sense that they own the Community Path. Thirdly, at 45 miles long, the sheer scale of the path is intimidating.

This book addresses the first problem by promoting a series of circular routes linking the Community Forest Path to places where people live or gather together, thus bringing the community to the Community Forest Path.

Secondly, the routes described in this book use the potential of the Community Forest Path to make links between parishes and unitary authorities. So, instead of being a thread running unseen alongside the communities around the periphery of the built up area surrounding Bristol, the Community Forest Path becomes part of a network linking communities to each other and to the countryside.

Lastly, the book breaks the path into manageable chunks. This is not a book for complete beginners, for whom the Sri Chinmoy Peace Mile in Eastville Park or the Easy Access Trails, promoted by South Gloucestershire Council would make a suitable starting point. Instead, it provides a series of achievable goals for people who have already begun to take exercise by walking or running and are wondering what to do next.

This volume deals with the network of paths within the circle of the Community Forest Path, which lead out from centres of population. A second volume is in the process of production, which will extend the network further into the surrounding villages.

Many of the routes in this book began as runs rather than walks. I have had the pleasant task of leading groups of runners into the countryside from a different pub every Thursday for a dozen years. That is how I built up the body of knowledge necessary to write this book. But a route that can be run can just as easily be walked. The main differences are the time that needs to be devoted to a route, and the number of refreshment breaks that can be taken on the way. A route that might be suitable for an evening run after work, with time for a swift pint afterwards, might take all day if you walked it, especially if you stop for lunch and a pint on the way.

These differences are illustrated by the triangular trail from Snuff Mills, which has two versions: a slightly longer route for walkers, which allows for a visit to a pub in each of the three corners: and a quicker route, which cuts the corners. In every case, walkers have the advantage when it comes to the opportunities for social contacts that make it a community path.

On the other hand, both runners and walkers can equally well enjoy the Forest. Forty two woods, copses, plantations and nature reserves are visited by the eighteen trails described in this book. In addition, the routes cross thirty four parks, downs, golf courses, recreation grounds and other green open spaces and pass twenty rivers, lakes, streams and ponds.

However, a mere enumeration of features can be misleading, because nature reserves tend to cluster around areas of need. One of the best trails through the countryside has only one river, two small stretches of wood and a viewpoint to list in its favour. Trails in the true countryside differ from more urban trails in this respect.

USING THE BOOK

To get the best out of this book, it should be used in combination with the Ordnance Survey Maps for Bristol. Most of the routes are covered by Explorer Map number 155, but number 167 (Thornbury, Dursley and Yate) is necessary for the northern section. Number 154 (Bristol and Portishead) is helpful for the 'Shopping' route. I have also found the Bristol A-Z for Bristol extremely useful.

It is possible to navigate all the routes using the book alone, and the sketch maps and instructions are as accurate as I could make them, but you should be aware that there is a general policy in train to replace stiles with kissing gates to make the footpaths more accessible. This is not the only potential source of errors, for which we can accept no liability. However, please inform the publishers of any mistakes you do find, so that they may be corrected in future editions.

The most up to date information about your rights and obligations in the countryside can be found at www.countrysideacess.gov.uk

There, you will find that there are now five sections to what used to be called The Country Code:

Be safe - plan ahead and follow any signs

Leave gates and property as you find them

Protect plants and animals and take your litter home

Keep dogs under close control

Consider other people.

More details about each of these can be found at the above website, which contains such information as: You are responsible for own safety; Check the weather before you go out; and so on. If you want to attempt the whole of the Community Forest Path, a free map is obtainable from www.forestofavon.org.uk, which also carries details of many other routes.

2: WESTBURY ON TRYM
OR 'THE RABBIT' 8M (approx.)
From the White Lion, Passage Road, W-O-T

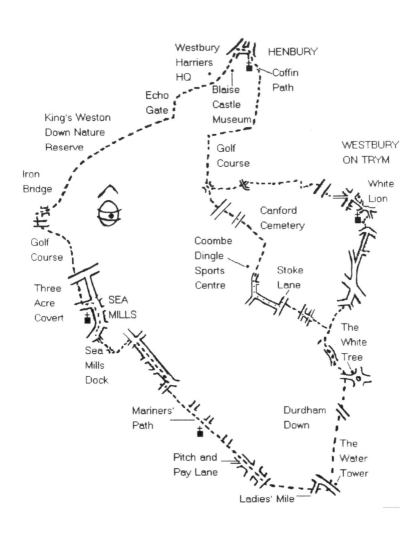

The shape that has emerged from this route map looks like a demented rabbit, but it should really be a hare, because this is the stamping ground of Westbury Harriers. Since 1891, the word 'harrier' has been used to describe 'one of a hare and hounds team' as in the game, also known as a paper chase, which was invented in 1845. Nowadays, serious running clubs, like Westbury Harriers, rarely, if ever, play 'hare and hounds', a version of which is now the preserve of several groups of 'hash house harriers' in the Bristol area. However, old photographs, which used to hang in the White Lion in Westbury, where the club was formed as a breakaway group from Bristol Athletic Club, suggest that it used to be otherwise. In 1924, Westbury was a village that maintained something of its identity as a rural settlement outside Bristol. However, it must have already accumulated a large population to justify the formation of a separate athletic club. Indeed, Westbury has always been an important centre. When Bristol was still part of the bishopric of Worcester, Westbury and Henbury were his preferred stopping places, and there was a brief moment when it was Westbury, rather than Bristol might have become the senior church.

Apart from the White Lion, which is a Harvester, there are numerous pubs, cafés and restaurants in Westbury, which make it an important social centre. We are particularly fond of the Victoria in Chock Lane, but other pubs have their advocates, including the Black Swan and the Prince of Wales in Stoke Lane. If you have a driver, there is a free car park in the village.

If you prefer to use public transport, the importance of Westbury is reflected in the fact that the number 1 bus joins Westbury and Bristol, as well as the 20, 21 and 55. It is also worth considering the subsidised train service from Temple Meads to Avonmouth, which can turn out cheaper than the bus. This stops at Sea Mills, a hundred metres from the Forest Path. There are two main variations on this route. The first starts at the White Lion, because it is easy to find at the end of the High Street. The second starts at the University Sports

Centre at Coombe Dingle, where Westbury Harriers train during the winter.

FROM THE WHITE LION TO THE WHITE TREE

From the pub, turn left and left again up Trym Road.

On the right is the back of Westbury College on the other side of the River Trym. This was the home of a college of canons, built by the bishop of Worcester.

Take the second turning on the right (Chock Lane) and turn right up the footpath to the church, just before the Victoria.

At the top of some steps, turn left along the footpath around the churchyard and then left again to emerge on Eastfield Road, just above The Mouse.

Cross the main road into the road opposite (also called Eastfield Road) and follow it until it joins Westbury Road at the top of Westbury Road (just above the Post Office tavern).

Keep going straight on up Westbury Road, past Redmaids' School until you reach a pedestrian crossing.

Cross the zebras across Westbury and Falcondale Roads onto the right hand pavement of Downs Road.

Follow the line of this pavement across the top of Great Brockerage to enter an enclosed footpath, which passes through the grounds of Badminton School.

Go straight ahead over two stone stiles at the bottom of Cote Lane.

FROM COOMBE DINGLE SPORTS CENTRE TO COTE LANE

From the sports centre, find the back entrance into Red House Lane.

Turn right and then second left up Stoke Grove to Stoke Lane.

Turn left* and then right up a footpath between the houses.

*(*The Black Swan and the Prince of Wales are c. 300m further up Stoke Lane.)*

At the end of the path, carry straight on across three roads to the drive leading into Elmlea Junior School.

Carry on up past the entrance to the school on a path that leads up a few steps to emerge at the bottom of a lane with stone stiles on either side. Take the right hand stile.

Over the stone stile, follow the path as it descends toward Elmlea School and around the bottom of some old people's homes.

When the path divides, turn left up to the bottom of a lane, which leads up to the edge of the Downs.

At the top, bear right and cross one road onto a section of the Downs that is usually allowed to grown into a meadow.

To the left is the White Tree Roundabout, which is named after the tree, which was painted white to guide a drunken resident home. Unfortunately, the original tree was an elm. Fortunately, it has been replaced.

FROM THE WHITE TREE TO THE WESTBURY TRYM

Cross another road onto the main section of the Downs, where you should be able to make out the shape of the Water Tower past the last of the pine trees that were known as the Severn Sisters. (Their replacements are growing nearby.) Head toward the Water Tower.

There are a café and toilets on either side of the Water Tower if you should need them.

From the Water Tower, cross the Stoke Road and bear right to cross Ladies' Mile, aiming to join the metalled footpath across the Downs to Julian Road.

The Ladies in question are the questionable ladies, who used to promenade along the road in the hope of intercepting the mariners who made their way up Mariners' Walk on their way into town.

Follow the line of the path across the road around the edge of the Downs and down Julian Road to Pitch and Pay Lane.

Julian Road is an allusion to the roman road, which is believed to have run nearby from Abona (Sea Mills). Pitch and Pay Lane is a reference to the tents and caravans of the ladies of the night. The houses along there now look very much more respectable.

When you cross the road at the end of Pitch and Pay Lane, you are on Mariners' Walk, which is the name of an old path from the dock at Sea Mills.

On Mariners' walk, look out for badger holes on the stretch before the church of St Mary Magdalene, and an atrocious rubbly surface on the section between the church and Druid Road. The brown flowers that look dead along this stretch are Ivy Broomrape, a root parasite on ivy. The last section of the path is comfortable going, if you don't mind conkers underfoot.

At the end of the path, turn right and first left - there is a short footpath that cuts the corner.

Keep to the left on the next section, which lacks a pavement. Follow the pavement down to the bottom of the hill when you find it.

Cross Sea Mills Lane onto the grass, and turn left beside the chestnut trees towards the old harbour.

Turn right across the footbridge over the weir.

Before you do this, it is worth going under the road bridge to look at the ruin of the Victorian Dock. It is only used by a few small pleasure boats, but was once a base for whaling ships. There are usually a few mallard in the harbour. And you can often see waders, if you carry on under the railway bridge to the bank of the River Avon.

You could start the route from here, if you caught the subsidised train from Temple Meads to Avonmouth, which stops at the platform beside the level crossing.

On the other side of the footbridge, bear right to find a footpath through the bushes.

Follow the path into a cul-de-sac and out onto Riverleaze.

Turn right and follow, Riverleaze past Sea Mills Junior School and St Edyth's Parish Church.

Turn left after the church and then right down a footpath into Three Acre Covert.

It can be difficult to follow this path during the late summer when the nettles and brambles are at their worst.

When the path emerges onto Sylvan Way, turn right and then left through a kissing gate onto Shirehampton Golf Course.

Keep to the right hand edge to avoid interfering with the golfers until you emerge through a kissing gate into Shirehampton Road.

Cross the road carefully and make your way to the Iron Bridge at the top of the grassy bank.

There is a folly belonging to Kingsweston House up some steps straight ahead. Refreshments are available at the Vaulted Tearoom on the other side of the house, which is three hundred and fifty metres further on down an avenue of trees.

If you do not need any refreshment yet - or if you have returned from the Tearoom - cross the Iron Bridge onto Kings Weston Hill and follow the clearing along the top of the ridge to the remains of a kissing gate at the corner of an earthen fort. Descend the steps through the trees on the other side of the gate and carry on, on the same line, until you emerge onto the grass at the spot marked Echo Gate on the relevant maps.

The gate no longer exists, but Issue 3 of the Blaise News shows a picture of it in 1930. (See echo-gate, blaise *on the web.)*

From the site of the gate, bear left around the edge of the trees ahead and head across the grass toward Blaise Castle House Museum.

There is another chance to sample the wares of Kingsweston House at the café between the car park and children's play equipment on the left. This modern café is run by the same people as Kingsweston House and the Café on the Downs by the Water Tower. There are also toilets here. The pavilion surrounded by the new playground is the HQ of Westbury Harriers.

Go past the entrance to the museum and out through the gate.

The pub nearly opposite is the Blaise Inn, which, the last time I visited it, sold rough cider. I was happy about this, but others in the party were less impressed.

Turn right (coming out of the gate) and right again down Church Lane.

At the end, turn right into the churchyard and bear left around the church.

One of the stones marks the famous grave of the slave-boy, Scipio. Less famous is the grave of Amelia Edwards who started the Egyptian Exploration fund. Her grave is marked by the ancient Egyptian symbol of life the **ankh,** *which bears only a superficial resemblance to a Christian cross.*

Pass the steps at the east end of the church unless you want to visit the Toby Carvery at the Salutation.

Just around the corner, another set of steps lead underground beside a yew tree.

This tunnel marks the end of the coffin path along which sailors from Sea Mills used to carry those of their companions who would never again be able to walk along the Mariners' Path to visit the ladies on the Downs.

Follow the coffin path through the tunnel, over the footbridge across the Hazel Brook and up the steps into a meadow.

Bear right across the grass along a path which climbs some steps to emerge next to a quirky cottage covered in bark.

Turn right past the cottage and then left up a track that leads through a rhododendron shrubbery and along the edge of a cliff.

Keep right, always bearing in mind the presence of the cliff. After the path has followed a wall between the golf course on your left and a steep beech wood on your right keep on the path that swings first right and then left to join a steeply descending enclosed track between the woods on the right and some fields on the left.

At the bottom of the track, watch out for some steps and turn left at the bottom alongside the River Trym.

Cross the river by means of a footbridge into a meadow.

FROM THE RIVER TRYM TO THE SPORTS CENTRE

In the meadow, turn right and look for a path up to the left, which leads up some steps to emerge beside some flats.

Turn right to the road and then left to a bus stop.

Cross the road and go down a track between the houses, across one road and through some allotments to a path that leads beside a cemetery.

Turn right beside the kissing gate into the cemetery.

Follow this path between the grass and all weather pitches of the Coombe Dingle Sports Complex into Red House Lane and turn right into the Complex.

In the meadow, turn left to a kissing gate and follow the path above the Trym until you emerge through a wood onto a metalled drive.

Go straight across to the metal footbridge over the stream Caution! It has no handrail!

Over the bridge, turn right through the meadow to a stile into Henbury Golf Course.

Follow the left hand edge of the fairway alongside a narrow wood and look for a path up through the trees.

Turn right along the other side of the wood. The path crosses a fairway to another stile. Watch out for golfers playing uphill from the right.

Over the stile, turn right and then left along an enclosed path. After about 150m, cross the steam by a footbridge and carry on up some steps to emerge alongside Falcondale Road.

Turn right and then left to a footpath to the right of the petrol station opposite. You will probably want to make use of the traffic lights to get there.

At the end of the path, go straight on into the cul de sac (Westfield Road) and follow it into the High Street.

The White Lion is to the left on the other side of the road.

3: SHOPPING
OR 'THE HENPECKED HUSBAND' 7 M
From Cribbs Causeway retail park

This poor fellow has been reduced to jelly by spending too long sitting outside cubicles in ladies' dress shops waiting to be asked his opinion. What should he say? Should he say what he thinks or what his wife wants him to think? And how is he supposed to know the difference? Perhaps he should make a break for it? When you are unwillingly stuck in the Regional Shopping Centre, doesn't the countryside look inviting?
If you park in the Retail Park car park, you can slip beside, beneath and behind the new development to gain a glimpse of Filton Airfield and British Aerospace beyond. If you look

carefully among the brambles along the perimeter fence, you might even discover the remains of Charlton village, which was flattened to extend the runway to accommodate the Bristol Brabazon in 1949. It is a shame that this giant white elephant did not get very far!

Once it gets across the M4 on the Forest trail, the route picks up the woods along Spaniorum Hill, Easter Compton and a new wood planted under the auspices of the Forest of Avon. There are fine views across to Wales from Spaniorum Hill, but also from the embankment alongside the motorway.

If you want to use public transport, there are about 20 buses to choose from. The most direct from the centre of Bristol is the no.1. But most people live elsewhere. The 43 and 43A also connect with Kingswood and Warmley and the 54 and 54A will bring you from Stockwood. The 43 and its allies bring in Bradley Stoke and the 75 will bring you from Hartcliffe. The 318 and 319 will bring you from Keynsham and Bath. The 482 will even bring you from Chipping Sodbury and Yate.

Refreshments are available in the Mall, at Morrisons and at Asda as well as the Venue. There is also the Fox at Easter Compton en route if you think you can get away with it!

FROM THE RETAIL PARK TO NORTON'S FARM

From the entrance to the Retail Park, go straight ahead to the far left corner.

Slip left and then right on the path around the corner.

At the top of the path, turn right and keep to the cycle/footpath as it goes round the backs of the underground car park to emerge through an underpass by Burger King at the Venue.

Turn left and follow the path to the left of Burger King up to the access road.

Cross the access road to a kissing gate.

Through the gate, bear left up the slope and then turn right along the edge of a plateau to the corner of the field.

In the corner, keep up on top of the ridge as paths descend on either side.

At the end, descend toward a road.

Before the road, turn left and then bear left to the top of the landscape feature.

This piece , which is supposed to represent an aero engine, provides an excellent viewpoint for looking over the airfield.

At the far side, go down the ridge toward a signpost ahead.

Continue past the post to the corner of the field by the airfield boundary.

Follow the boundary fence to a wicket gate at the bottom of Catbrain Lane.

Go straight ahead to a kissing gate into a field.

In the field, turn right along the right hand hedge to find a two-stile bridge over the stream on the right. Watch out, there is tricky ditch in the way!

Over the stream, go straight up the hill to a kissing gate onto a tarmac path.

Follow the path between warehouses and new homes onto Cribbs Causeway.

Turn left and cross the dual carriageway by the pedestrian lights and turn left along the cycle/footpath.

Follow the path past a petrol station, Saracens' Ground and Clifton Rugby Club to find Berwick Lane on the right.

Go up the lane to Norton's Farm, where the Forest Trail joins from the left.

FROM NORTON'S FARM TO THE BANANA BRIDGE

Follow the lane uphill, round Haw Wood and over the motorway (M5).

The OS map is wrong at this point. The path goes up the lane to a crossroads.

At the crossroads, turn right down a track and then turn left through a kissing gate into a field beside a wood.

Keeping the wood on your left, follow the field edge past a double stile and then go straight on until the path goes through a short section of scrubby wood.

Through the kissing gate into the next field, keep going on the same line through an open gateway and two kissing gates across a new fenced track into another field (above Spaniorum Farm).

In this field, admire the views to your left and bear slightly right along the edge of the escarpment to a kissing gate in the hedge corner.

In next field, head downhill to a wicket gate in the opposite corner.

Continue to descend with a hedge on your right through a kissing gate. Through yet another kissing gate, the path goes past an orchard to a kissing gate and steps onto a tarmac road. In the road, turn right and then left down an enclosed path through a kissing gate into a field.

In the field, bear right to a kissing gate.

Keep going towards the church.

The path goes straight through the graveyard into a field.

Go straight ahead across the field to a kissing gate by a car park.

Go straight ahead to a road.

(The Fox Inn is about forty metres to the left if you are feeling thirsty!)

In the road, turn right and then left down a drive to a cycle trap ahead.

Keep going past a playground to find a double-stile in the corner on the right opposite some skate board ramps.

Over this stile, go straight ahead to find a pair of kissing gates to cross a farm track into a new plantation.

This is the Wheat Hill Farm plantation mentioned on the Forest of Avon Website.

In the wood, bear left to a double stile into a field, (There is a disused stile immediately to the right after the double-stile.) and then bear right to another double stile in the opposite corner of the field.

Over the double stile, go diagonally right to another double stile by a telegraph pole (with power lines).

In the next field, bear diagonally right to find double hunting gates over a bridge.

Turn immediately right to a badly maintained stile with a new gate on the other side.

Bear left to a wobbly stile beside a gate in the diagonally opposite corner of the field.

Keep going on the same line to find a stile into an orchard and another onto a metalled road.

Over the road take the stile into an enclosed path.

At the end take the stile on the left into another enclosed path and then a stile onto a lane.

Turn right and continue up the lane to a junction with a major road.

Turn left and then right up an enclosed path, through a wood (Pegwell Brake) and across another field to emerge on a footbridge over the motorway (M5).

FROM THE BANANA BRIDGE TO THE RETAIL PARK

Over the bridge, bear right along the path, which runs along top of the bank that acts as a noise barrier to the motorway traffic.

The path descends to a green area between some factories and the motorway.

This is the Eagle Field, mentioned in the Patchway Greenway leaflet. Apparently a Roman Road was discovered in the field.

Keep straight ahead until you see a scorched post and rail fence and a broken stone path to the left.

Follow the path over a footbridge into the ASDA car park.

Go straight ahead along the car park road.

As the road bends to the right, follow the path up the bank ahead to the public road.

Turn right on the grass verge alongside the road to a pavement leading to a pedestrian crossing.

Over the crossing, turn right to a road junction.

Cross two carriageways to a pedestrian crossing.

Cross the dual carriageway using the crossing.

On the far side, turn right and then left across a footbridge.

Keep going alongside the ornamental river on your left.

Cross a side road into the path between the ornamental river and Morrison's car park.

Cross the wooden footbridge over the ornamental river. This probably represents the original source of Hazel Brook, with silicone implants!

Over the bridge, use the pedestrian lights to cross to return to the Retail Park car park.

4: PATCHWAY AND BRADLEY STOKE
OR 'THE MOUSE DEER' 6M
From the Traveller's Rest, Gloucester Road, Patchway

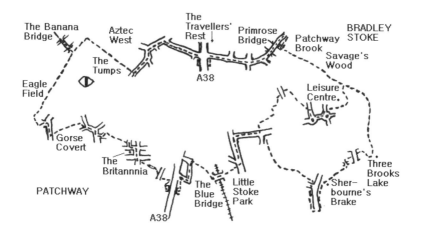

This strange, sad creature appears to have been assembled in the course of a failed genetic experiment. Its appearance is not deceptive, because this route has been cobbled together from two published routes, 'The Patchway Greenway' and 'The Three Brooks Walk', which is based in Bradley Stoke. It also suffers from the fact that it is trapped by the M4/M5 junction and cut up by the A38 and the main railway line to Wales.

The Community Path was seduced onto this unpromising ground by The Greenway, which was one of the first projects supported by the Forest of Avon. The pamphlet describing the route, which is still obtainable at Patchway Council offices, is beginning to show its age. It is printed in two colours in a folded A2 format, and the route can no longer be followed in its entirety, due to building work in Bradley Stoke. On the other hand, 'The Three Brooks Walk', described in a glossy eighteen page booklet with full-colour pictures, shows evidence of more generous funding.

31

However, both 'The Three Brooks Walk' and the 'Community Forest Path' owe an unacknowledged debt to the Greenway that preceded them. It was surely the Greenway that attracted the Forest Path away from its obvious course through Almondsbury and Gaunt's Earthcott, and the Three Brooks walk would have been inconceivable without it. Combining the two gives us the best of both worlds, with a total of three woods - four if you count a near miss at Webb's Wood, several ponds and, of course, three brooks.

The route provides a link between the two communities. A group setting out on a fraternal visit to Patchway from Bradley Stoke would probably assemble at the leisure centre and repair afterwards to the Three Brooks. A similar group from Patchway meet at the council offices opposite the Britannia Inn. But a stranger would do better to start and finish at the Travellers' rest on the A38, since it is a lot easier to find, although you will have to make a circuit around the Aztec West roundabout to get to it if you are travelling from Bristol by car. The 73 and 75 buses go to Patchway and Bradley Stoke, but their routes are complicated and it advisable to check with the bus companies before setting out!

FROM THE TRAVELLERS' REST TO BRAYDON AVENUE

According to the Greenway pamphlet, this was a New Inn in 1800, when it was built as a coaching inn on the turnpike. It is now a 'Hungry Horse'.

From the pub, turn left and left again down 'The Common' *(the source of a quarter of the entries in the original pamphlet).*

Cross Brook Way into The Common East *(now an isolated fragment of Patchway jutting into Bradley Stoke.)*

At the end of this road cross Bradley Stoke Way by means of the Primrose Bridge (a footbridge named after a demolished cottage) and turn right at the other side back towards the Patchway Brook.

At this point, the Forest Path and the original Patchway

Greenway diverge. The Forest Path crosses the Brook to follow the right bank, while the Greenway follows the left. Since this is a loop off the Forest Path we prefer to follow the right bank.

Continue along the path with the stream on your left, through a recent example of the hedge layer's art and a new pond into Savage's Wood.

It is said that this 'may be a fragment of the ancient forest that covered Britain after the last Ice Age.

Go across a bridge over a ditch and veer left towards a stile and kissing gate out of the wood.

A DUBIOUS SHORTCUT

When you leave the wood, take the first turning on your right, which leads along a cycle track between the wood and some playing fields.

The first turning on your right takes you into the car park of Bradley Stoke Leisure Centre and Library.

From the Library, cross Bradley Stoke way and go along Savage's Wood Road to the Three Brooks public House. *I see the right of way has been diverted to avoid going through the pub; but I see no reason why you should not enter the pub for old times' sake!*

Turn right at the pub towards Tesco and look for footpath on the left. **As things stand at the moment (March 2006), you can follow the hedge to a tarmac path off to the right beside Dewfall's Pond.**

In the road, turn left through the houses of Dewfalls Drive to emerge in Brook Way.

Cross the road at pedestrian crossing and follow path between the houses opposite.

Turn left to emerge in a grassy space and then turn right behind some tennis courts.

In the open, head for the diagonally opposite corner of a playing field to emerge at the junction between Braydon Avenue and Savage's Wood Road.

Turn right down Braydon Avenue.

Go straight ahead on the cinder track to Three Brooks Lake. Turn right by the lake and follow the cycle track under Bradley Stoke Way. (Webb's Wood is up to the right before the bridge.) Just after the overhead bridge, turn left over Stoke Brook and then turn right into Sherbourne's brake, a woodland strip alongside the brook.

Out of the wood, turn right to Bailey's Court Road and right again up Brook Way until a foot/cycle path joins from the right.

Turn left, cross Brook Way and follow the path beside the brook on the far side of the road.

When the path reaches Savage's Wood Road, turn left into Braydon Avenue.

FROM BRAYDON AVENUE TO THE BANANA BRIDGE

At the end of Braydon Avenue, turn left down Little Stoke Lane until you can turn right into a large playing field.

Turn right and head for the left hand hedge of a fenced off football pitch, where you will find a path leading to a footbridge over the railway line.

Over the bridge follow path into a field with extremely emphatic waymarks to keep you from straying from the right of way.

Over a stile, follow path into a road and turn left.

Follow road round a bend to the right and then turn left down a back alleyway and look out for a ramp down under the A38 on the right.

Through the tunnel, turn north past a bank and across Callicroft Road to look foe a footpath on the left past Flingers, the party shop.

Go straight across Hazeldene Road into another path past some garages into a triangular 'square' with a green in the middle.

Keep left to another lane past some derelict and bricked up garages to emerge near a dual carriageway (Highwood Road). Cross the carriageway by the traffic lights and go down

Durban Road between the library and the fire station.

Turn left past the Britannia public house and then right down Worthing Road to look for a lane to the left. *(The Greenway sign pointing to the right indicates a short cut to Aztec West through Norman Scott Park. The division of the Greenway into East and West 'halves' at this point is probably another reason why the Patchway Greenway concept is not very popular in Bradley Stoke.)*

Follow the back lane, taking a right fork, until you can turn left into Lee Close and then right into Cavendish Road beside a junior school.

Turn left down Stroud Road then left again into Brighton Road.

Take the second snicket on the right into a green open space. Go straight ahead until a path on the left leads to a kissing gate into a wood called Gorse Covert. *This used to be a fox covert owned by the Berkeley Hunt. It is now preserved as a nature reserve.*

There are a number of paths in Gorse Covert. You need to keep straight ahead as much as possible to emerge in Coniston Road.

Turn right until you can take the left horn of Eagle Drive, which leads eventually into an open space through a gate.

This is the Eagle Field, so called because a Roman road was discovered under it. It has survived somehow when the rest of it was wiped out by the M5. It is mainly used by youths with motorcycles, who risk the confiscation of their machines by the police. I cannot see what harm they are doing there. The noise cannot be a factor so close to the motorway!

Turn right in the Eagle Field and make your way over a stile and onto the embankment beside the motorway. *The noise is terrible but there are tremendous views across the Severn to Wales.*

If you want respite from the noise of the traffic, you can descend some steps to a playground and carry on below the embankment on a parallel path.

This path is only parallel in a non-Euclidian sense as it soon rejoins the path on the embankment, which in turn joins the Forest Path by the aptly named Banana Bridge over the motorway from Pegwell Brake.

FOREST PATH FROM THE BANANA BRIDGE TO THE A38

Do not cross the Banana Bridge. Instead, follow the Forest Path straight on and then round a ninety-degree bend to the right.

To the right is Turner's Pond, which is well looked-after by local conservation volunteers and worth a diversion.

Follow the left hand fence (through a cycle trap) until you can go no further.

The strip of land is called the Tumps because of the mounds to the right of the path, which runs along the top of the tunnel of the main railway line from Bristol to South Wales. The Tumps are the spoil left by the tunnelers.

At the end of the Tumps is a cross road, called Waterside Drive. *(The short cut across Norman Scott Park rejoins the main Greenway at this point from the direction of the BMX track opposite.)*

Turn left into the Aztec West estate and follow the path around the lake to Park Avenue.

Turn right and follow the road past one road to some steps down to the right.

These lead you into Hempton Lane, which emerges past Patchway School onto the A38.

To regain the Travellers Rest, turn right and right again into an underpass that emerges on the other side to the south of The Common.

Cross the Common, and return to the pub.

5: THE RATEPAYERS' ARMS
OR 'THE JANUS-BEAST' 14.5M
From Filton Recreation Centre

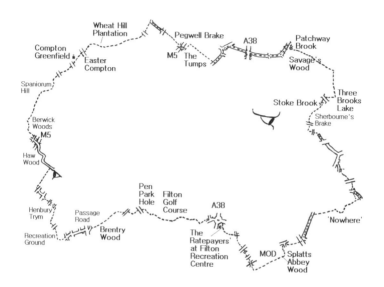

This ferocious looking double headed beast represents a challenging route of nearly fifteen miles around the Four Towns of Filton, Patchway, Bradley Stoke and Stoke Gifford. I have included it because it brings together the whole of the northern section of the Forest Path.

It starts from the Ratepayers' Arms, which is part of the Filton Recreation Centre. This has more than adequate parking unless there is a football tournament in progress on the playing fields. In addition, this is probably the only recreation centre in the British Isles with a mention in The Good Beer Guide. This is a bonus, since there are few pubs on or close to this section of the Forest Path. (The Wayfarer on Pen Park Road is on the route, as is the Salutation at Henbury, and the Hungry Horse is visible from the path on the A38. The Fox at Easter Compton is not far away either.) But the route is too long for a pub-crawl in any case!

From the forestal point of view, the route adds Splatts Abbey Wood and a linear wood at Brentry, as well as three sports grounds and a golf course, which all support wildlife of one sort or another.

The Filton Recreation Centre is behind the police station in Gloucester Road North. Several buses stop at the police station, including the 75, 75A, 99, 309, 319 and517.

FROM FILTON TO HENBURY

From the entrance to Ratepayers Arms in the Filton Recreation Centre Car Park, turn right towards the playing fields.

On the tarmac path turn left and left again to the footbridge ramp.

Do not cross the footbridge, but carry on down the ramp toward the roundabout.

Cross Gloucester Road and turn right and then left down Southmead Road.

Cross the road by the traffic lights into Golf Course Lane.

In the lane turn left onto the footpath around the car park.

Keep to the footpath around the offices and alongside the chain-link fence around the factory buildings to emerge on Filton Golf Course.

On the course, turn right and then left on the line of a sunken drain.

On the far side, turn right uphill and then left through a gap in the hedge into another section of the course.

Follow the left hand hedge to a kissing gate on the left at the top of the hill.

Through the kissing gate, turn right on a tarmac path through a green at the back of some houses.

Follow the path through a cycle trap and bear left through the park to emerge by a hunting gate onto Penpark Road. *The notorious cave, Penpark Hole is hidden in the bushes in this little park. It is an enormous cavern, considered too dangerous for public access. At least one vicar fell in and drowned before it was sealed.*

Cross the road and go through the kissing gate into the field opposite.

There is a pub off to the right at this point, called The Wayfarer, but it is bit early for a refreshment break.

In the field, bear right to a gap in the hedge.

Turn right to emerge on Charlton Road through a kissing-gate in the right hand corner of the field.

Turn left and cross the road-crossing to a tarmac path on the right.

Follow the path down hill and round to the left.

Keep straight ahead ignoring a path and a track on your right to emerge on a green at the back of some houses.

Turn left where two paths cross into a wood.

Bear right on a cinder path through the wood.

Ignore kissing gates on the right and continue straight on until the path emerges at the top of some steps in a green open space.

This wood has only recently been opened up to the public. The green open space used to belong to Brentry Hospital, but access has been opened up since part of the hospital grounds was sold for housing.

Descend the steps to find a hole in the wall and turn right to a dual carriageway.

Cross this road carefully and go down Dragonswell Road.

At a T-junction, turn right and then first left down Challender Avenue.

At the end of this road, go straight ahead past some flats onto some playing fields.

Go around the top edge of a fenced football pitch and then turn right to a cycle path down the hill, which emerges in a busy road (Crow Lane).

The Salutation is off to the left at this point if you need a drink.

Cross Crow Lane into an open space and follow the path towards a stream (the Henbury Trym).

Just before a footbridge over the stream, turn right along a muddy path.

FOREST PATH FROM HENBURY TO THE A38

Continue along muddy path until you reach a footbridge over the stream.

Over the footbridge, bear right across the grass to a cul-de-sac.

Follow the road to a T-junction and turn right.

Turn left down a path between the houses to emerge on a main road.

In road turn right and then left over some traffic calming bumps.

Turn right on the pavement and then left down Greenlands Way and left again down Greenlands Road.

At the junction with Meadowland Road, go straight ahead over a railway-bridge to kissing gate into a field.

Turn right and keeping a hedge on your right, go through three kissing gates, which take you through horse paddocks.

Keep along hedge until you emerge through a wicket gate into a lane opposite Norton Farm. (The OS map is inaccurate at this point.)

In Berwick Lane, turn left and follow the road round Haw Wood and over the motorway (M5).

The OS map is wrong at this point as well. The path goes up the lane to a crossroads.

At crossroads, turn right down a track and then left through a kissing gate into the field beside Berwick Wood.

(The OS map shows the wood extending to the motorway, which it does not, with the path entering the field (used for quad biking) beside the motorway.)

Keep following the field edge past a double stile and go straight on past the end of Berwick Wood through an empty gateway until the path goes through a scrubby copse.

Over the stile into the field beyond the copse, keep going on the same line through an open gateway and through two kissing gates across a new fenced track into another field (above Spaniorum Farm).

In this field, admire the views to the left and bear slightly right along the edge of the escarpment to a stile in a hedge corner.

In next field, head downhill to a stile in the opposite corner.

Continue to descend with a hedge on your right over another stile. Over yet another stile, the path goes past an orchard to a kissing gate and steps onto a tarmac road.

In the road, turn right and then left down an enclosed path through a kissing gate into a field.

In the field, bear right to a kissing gate.

Keep going towards the church.

The path goes straight through the graveyard into a field.

Go straight ahead across the field to a kissing gate by a car park.

Go straight ahead to a road.

(The Fox Inn is along the road to the right if you are feeling thirsty!)

In the road, turn right and then left down a drive to a cycle trap ahead.

Keep going past a playground to find a double-stile in the corner on the right opposite some skate board ramps.

Over this stile, go straight ahead to find a pair of kissing gates to cross a farm track into a new plantation.

This is the Wheat Hill Farm plantation mentioned on the Forest of Avon Website.

In the wood, bear left to a double stile into a field, (There is a disused stile immediately to the right after the double-stile.) and then bear right to another double stile in the opposite corner of the field.

Over the double stile, go diagonally right to another double stile by a telegraph pole (with power lines).

In the next field, bear diagonally right to find double hunting gates over a bridge.

Turn immediately right to a badly maintained stile.

Bear left to a gateway in the diagonally opposite corner of the field.

Keep going on the same line to find a stile into an orchard and another onto a metalled road.

Over the road take the stile into an enclosed path.

At the end take the stile on the left and follow another enclosed path to a stile onto a lane.

Turn right and continue up the lane to a junction with a major road.

Turn left and then right up an enclosed path, through a wood (Pegwell Brake) and across another field to emerge on a footbridge over the motorway (M5).

Over the bridge, turn left through a cycle trap into an enclosed path alongside motorway and then right down a path with Aztec West industrial estate on your left.

Go through another cycle trap and the path emerges into some playing fields.

Keep going on same line to a cycle trap to the left of a double field gate.

Through the trap, turn left through another cycle trap into Aztec West Business Park.

Follow the Brick Road to its junction with a tarmac road.

Turn left on the pavement alongside an ornamental lake to another road junction.

At this junction, turn right and follow the pavement over one junction to a footpath on the right, which descends some steps into a residential road.

Follow the road to emerge on the A38 next to Patchway Community College.

If you have overdone the walking, you have three options at this point.

You can take a shortcut back into Filton by turning right and walking back alongside Filton airfield (suitable for plane spotters).

You can cross the road via the underpass and look for a bus stop.

You can cross the road via the underpass and seek refreshment at the Hungry Horse and see how you feel after that!

FROM THE A38 TO 'NOWHERE'

From Patchway Community College, turn right and right again to cross the A38 by the underpass.

On the other side, re-orientate yourself to find The Common opposite the School.

Follow The Common across one crossroad by a pedestrian crossing and carry on down The Common (East) and across a footbridge over Bradley Stoke Way and the Patchway Brook.

Turn sharp right and keep right over a lesser footbridge and then turn left to follow the Patchway Brook along its right bank.

Go through the gap in a cut and laid hedge, across a metalled path from a bridge on the left and past a pond into Savage's Wood.

Go over a wooden bridge in the wood and bear left to a kissing-gate and stile out of the wood.

Keep going on a cinder track alongside Patchway Brook to the Three Brooks Lake.

This lake was formed by damming the Bradley Brook, which is formed by the confluence of the Patchway Brook and the Stoke Brook. Another brook, the Hortham Brook, joins the Patchway Brook through a culvert under the motorway just after Savage's Wood.

By the lake, turn right, keeping Stoke Brook on your left until it passes under a road-bridge overhead.

On the far side of the bridge, turn left over the brook and then right along a muddy woodland path, with the stream on your right.

Keep going through the wood (Sherbourne's Brake) until you cross Bailey's Court Road beside a roundabout.

After about100m, turn left down a path between some houses.

Cross one road and turn right at a junction to emerge at some pedestrian traffic lights on Winterbourne Road.

Over the road, carry on, on same line up Mead Road to its junction with North Road.

Turn right down North Road and left down Rocks Lane, which is the second on the left and is marked by a blue signpost to Parkway etc.

Before Rocks lane bends to the right, turn left and then right on a cycle path signed to Parkway and the University of the West of England.

Go straight on over Hunt's Ground Road, following signs to the University of West of England, until you emerge over a railway bridge onto a road.

Turn left down the road, to find a kissing gate on the right.

In the field, go straight on to another kissing gate.

Some new planting and fencing has confused matters here, and the line of the new hedge directs you to a kissing gate and a bridge. Do not be led astray. You need to turn right at this point to find a metal stile.

This is 'Nowhere', because, according the Stoke Gifford parish walk leaflet, this patch was left off parish maps.

FROM 'NOWHERE' TO THE RATEPAYERS' ARMS

Over the stile, follow a muddy path until it widens into a track.

Look for a kissing-gate into the field on your left.

Bear right across the field to a stile on your right onto a cycle path just before the top right hand corner of the field.

Turn left and carry straight ahead down Harry Stoke Road.

As the road bends sharply left, go straight ahead to the traffic lights over the ring-road to Hewlett Packard.

On the pavement, turn right then left down the footpath beside a pylon.

Turn left at a road junction and follow the path on the right to a kissing gate.

Follow the path beside Splatt's Abbey Wood to another gate

and go straight ahead on the cycle path between the M.O.D. enclosure on the right and a spare field belonging to Hewlett Packard on the left.

Turn right at end of M.O.D. security fence and right again until a path to your left leads through a cycle trap and over a railway-bridge.

Carry straight on over one road into a service road.

At a junction, turn right and then left down the path between the houses.

At the main road (Filton Avenue), bear right across the road to a path between the houses opposite.

The path leads into another service road, which you follow until you emerge in a road.

Turn left and carry straight ahead to a kissing gate and across the playing field back to Filton Recreation Centre and the Ratepayers Arms.

6: THE DOWER HOUSE
OR 'THE DUCHESS' 6M
From Snuff Mills car park, off Broom Hill, Stapleton

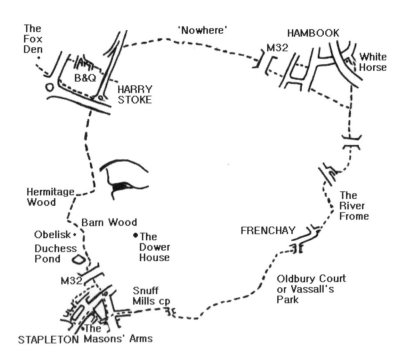

I was introduced to this route by former TACH member, Tony Fletcher, and I shall always think of it as Fletcher's Run. It only uses a short stretch of the Forest Path, but it has always been one of my favourites, perhaps because we do it as a circular run from the Mason's Arms in Stapleton, which serves at least three varieties of rough cider.

In the cause of sobriety and responsible parking, this version begins in the car park of Snuff Mills Park. However, I have also included loops at the three corners of the route to enable visits to the Mason's Arms Stapleton, the Fox Den in Harry Stoke and the White Horse in Hambrook.

The first part of the route enters the parish of Stoke Gifford beside the Dower House, whose yellow walls dominate the view of Purdown from the M32. It passes the Duchess Pond and goes though Barn Wood and Hermitage Wood before passing along a footpath between the UWE and the grounds of Hewlett Packard. It emerges close to the last coalmine sunk near Bristol between Abbey Wood and Hewlett Packard in 1953. This was known as the Harry Stoke Mine.

The route crosses the ring road into Harry Stoke before taking off across the fields. It leaves the parish of Stoke Gifford at the corner called 'Nowhere', where there is some new planting. A short stretch of the Forest Path takes us into Hambrook.

The return to Snuff Mills along the Frome passes outcrops of Pennant Sandstone, which are visible evidence of the coal measures, which provided the coal that powered the industry of the South Gloucestershire Coalfield. The stone was also used extensively in Victorian terraced houses in Bristol, often with more expensive Bath-stone details around the doors and windows.

FROM SNUFF MILLS TO HARRY STOKE

From Snuff Mills car park, return along River View to the main road (Broom Hill). *Note the smallest chapel in Bristol on the right.*

Either: turn right up Broom Hill to a mini-roundabout, cross over to the old gates into the Dower House and proceed straight ahead to the tunnel under the motorway.

Or: Cross Broomhill Road to a footpath alongside the river. Turn right up some steps. Go straight ahead at the top of the steps to the main road and turn left along the pavement to **the Masons' Arms**.

From the **Masons' Arms** turn left and then right past garage up Duchess Way.

Follow road round to right and look for Countess Walk on left.

Go up Countess Walk into green open space and turn right to find stile in far corner.

Over stile, go straight on down slope and then left to tunnel under motorway.

47

On the far side of the tunnel, turn right and then left across the grass beside the Duchess Pond to the obelisk at the top of Star Hill.

Look for a kissing gate into Barn Wood and bear left up through the wood to another kissing gate.

Bear left across the grass to the corner of Hermitage Wood and turn right along the covert side until you reach a wide track through the wood.

Follow the track, which crosses a stone bridge in the process of restoration, until you reach a cycle track on the far side.

Turn right past the back entrance to Hewlett Packard and turn left down the path between HP and the back of the University of WoE.

At the end of the path (by the front entrance to Hewlett Packard) turn right to the pedestrian crossing across the Ring Road.

The Harry Stoke Mine sunk in 1953 was the other side of the entrance to Hewlett Packard. It was a slope mine, but closed because the seams were more difficult to work than the initial bore holes had suggested.

FROM HARRY STOKE TO THE OLD GLOUCESTER ROAD

On the far side of the Ring Road

Either: Go straight on down Harry Stoke Road past one kissing gate on the right.

Or: Turn left alongside the Ring Road; pass Sainsbury; cross Great Stoke Way beside the roundabout and go past the Holiday Inn to **the Fox Den.**

From the Fox Den, return to Great Stoke Way and turn left to the pedestrian crossing.

Go up footpath on the other side, which emerges beside Sainsbury opposite B&Q.

Cross the road; turn left and then right past the entrance to B&Q into Fox Den Road.

Follow the left hand pavement to a tarmac path that leads between some houses to emerge in Harry Stoke Road.

Turn left.

On Harry Stoke Road, go straight on until you pass some farm buildings on your right and look for a stile into a field on your right.

Over the stile, bear left to a kissing gate at the far end of the field.

Through the gate, turn right and follow track (which becomes a muddy path) to a metal stile and turn right.

This is 'Nowhere' because it was not included in any parish in the tithe relief maps of the early nineteenth century. Note new planting on the left.

Go straight ahead, ignoring the path over a stream to your right, to a kissing gate.

Through the gate, carry on in the same direction to another kissing gate.

Keep going along the hedge on your right to a muddy corner, where you must turn right over a stile onto an enclosed path under the motorway.

Through the tunnel, climb a stile into a path alongside a stream which emerges on Old Gloucester Road.

FROM THE OLD GLOUCESTER ROAD TO SNUFF MILLS

Either: Cross the road into 'The Stream' and follow it to a main road.

Cross over to a stone stile between some houses into a field.
Go straight ahead in the field to a kissing gate up onto a path.
Turn left and look for a stile on the right, which descends to follow the brook to its confluence with the Frome.

This is presumably the eponymous Ham Brook, although its name is not marked on any map I can find.

Turn right alongside the River Frome.

Or: Turn left up the Old Gloucester Road and look for a footpath on the right (after about. 200m).

In the road, turn left and then right past **The Crown Inn** (rated 5.5/10 on the beerin theevening Website)) and under the motorway.

Turn right down Mill Lane past the **White Horse** (6.5/10) and the **Hambrook** (4.0/10).

At the bottom of Mill Lane, turn right to follow the River Frome walkway under the motorway bridge.

Alongside the Frome, continue to follow the river until your way ahead is blocked by a fence.

Turn right up a cinder track to a gate.

Past the gate, turn left up the drive to a road and turn right to emerge on Cleeve Road opposite a field known as Frenchay Moor.

Turn left across some grass past a stone tower that used to be a dovecote.

At the end of the grass, turn right across road to a kissing gate into field.

This is part of Frenchay Moor access land owned by the National Trust.

In the field, go straight ahead to find a gap in the fence on your left.

Through the gap, bear right past a wood to a stile in the bottom right hand corner of the field.

Over the stile, turn right and follow the path to stone stile into cul-de-sac. *Goldfinches feed on the alders along the river here during the winter months.*

At the other end of Chapel Lane, turn left and follow Frenchay Hill Road round a bend to the right to find a bridge over the River Frome on your left.

Over the bridge, turn right into Vassall's Park. *This heritage site is otherwise known as Oldbury Court Estate.*

In the park, turn right down some steps to the riverside.

Follow the river along a muddy, rocky path to emerge in a clearing.

If you are lucky, you may see a kingfisher along this stretch. You are more likely to see a grey wagtail or two and to hear the chattering of a jay in the oak trees up to the left.

Continue to follow the river along a metalled path to a bridge back over the Frome.

Over the bridge, turn left into Snuff Mills Park.

Follow metalled path around the restored buildings of the mill and into the car park

7: EMERSON'S GREEN
OR 'THE VAMPIRE' 7M
From Emerson's Green retail centre car park

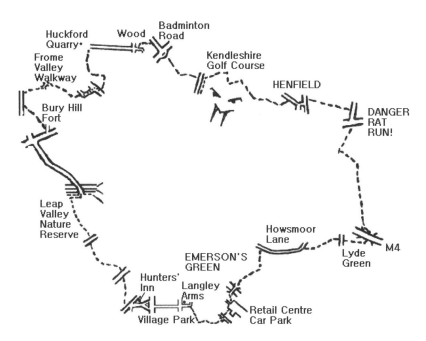

The spectre hovering over Emerson's Green is the threat to build a science park between the ring road and the motorway in the Howsmoor Lane area. This would doubtless attract welcome jobs to the area, but it would also cut off a valuable link between Emerson's Green and the countryside. Planning blight has already led to the abandonment of one footpath in the Lyde Green area.

It would be a shame if the link between Emerson's Green and the Forest Path were broken, because, on the whole, the planners have done a good job here. The old network of lanes and paths in Emerson's Green has been preserved across the grain of the road system to provide a safe environment for walkers, runners and cyclists, who make the most of these facilities, especially at the weekend.

The route starts at the Langley Arms a converted Farm building in the middle of new housing and heads out along one of the cycle ways to a footbridge over the ring road. It finds a green route out to Lyde Green where it joins the Community Forest Path, which tunnels under the motorway on the Dramway Path through the Parkfield and Coalpit Heath District of the South Gloucestershire Coalfield. Next the Forest Path crosses the Kendalshire Golf Course and finds a green route along the River Frome Walkway to Bury Hill, an Iron Age hill fort.

As an added bonus, the return link over the ring road follows the length of the Leap Valley Conservation area, a surprising green oasis through a built up area and the Emerson's Green Village Park.

There is plenty of parking at the Emerson's Green Retail Centre, which is also served by the 48, 49, 462, 518 and 686 buses.

Refreshments are available from the Hunters Inn and the Langley Arms en route, and there are several places where refreshments can be had in the Retail Centre, ranging from Sainsbury's café to the Millhouse and Botteloni's Italian restaurant.

FROM THE LANGLEY ARMS TO LYDE TUNNEL

Leave the car park between Boots and a skate board park, and turn right to find a footbridge over the ring road.

On the other side descend some steps to a stile into the field ahead.

Go straight ahead through the field, through a gap to a stile into a rising field.

Over the stile, carry on up the hill, passing Hallen Farm on your right onto a drive.

Turn left and follow it to Howsmoor Lane.

This is the heart of the proposed Science Park whose shadow has blighted this area.

Turn right and follow the lane through a small green just before the lane bends to the left.

Go straight ahead down a green path until it crosses a boggy area by means of a sleeper bridge.

The area to the left is the place where the shadow of the Science Park has had the greatest effect. The field on the left and the next field are marked on the map as access land, but it is not in fact possible to cross it on the footpaths marked on the OS map. The reason for this is that the right of way officers are put off by the fact that the Science will be built some time.

Go straight on across the rough grazing to a stile onto Gypsy Lane.

Cross the lane to a gate into the next field and cross the field as best as you can to diagonally opposite corner. This field is usually arable, so it is probably better to follow the rows of the crops rather than trying to keep to the exact line of the right of way.

Your target is a tunnel under the motorway, where you join the Community Forest Path and the Dramway.

Ahead, you can see the chimney of Parkfield Colliery and the remains of a slagheap. Most of the slagheap has been carried away for road ballast, but you can still see where it used to stand.

FROM THE LYDE GREEN TUNNEL TO BURY HILL

The first part of this section follows the line of the Dramway footpath.

If the gate in the tunnel is shut there are steps to the left. There is a wicket gate to the left of the field gate at the far end of the tunnel. (Watch out! You can bark your shins here if you are careless.) Turn left after the wicket gate through another field gate.

Go straight ahead and then turn right to a kissing gate keeping a wire fence on your left.

Keep going straight ahead to a double-stile-bridge.

Keep going, on same line through a gap to a field gate, which is usually tied with barbed wire.

Three roe deer ran away from me to the right the last time I used this path.

Through (or over) the gate, bear diagonally left, past a thicket in the middle of field to a kissing gate.

The thicket conceals the disused mineshaft of probably Parkgate Colliery an outlier of Parkfield Colliery, which was owned by Handel Cossham who built Cossham Hospital for miners on Lodge Hill in Kingswood. He was a noted philanthropist and thirty thousand people attended his funeral.

Turn right in the bridle path opposite a strange device for exercising horses and continue to Westerleigh Road.

Warning! This road is a rat run and carries a great deal more traffic than is reasonable!

After carefully crossing Westerleigh Road, continue down the lane opposite to some cottages on the left.

Follow the path down the drive to a horse gate into a field.

Keep going along the hedge on the right to a kissing gate, to a narrower one in a horse fence and to another kissing gate onto the road at Henfield.

Here the Forest Path leaves the Dramway path, which continues up to the right towards Coalpit Heath. On the way it passes Bitterwell Lake, where mine owners used to soak pit props for reasons of their own. It is now a popular venue for carp fishermen.

On the road, turn left and then right at a junction.

Keep going past the first junction on the left and look for a stile onto a golf course on the left.

On the golf course, follow the drive to the car parks.

Turn right, through the first car park to find a cinder track, which follows the edge of the course to the Half Way Halt café.

Keep on the track as it bends to the right to a field gate.

Turn left just before the gate and follow the path alongside the road past two gates to a kissing gate onto Ruffet Road.

On the road, turn right to find a gate onto the section of the golf course on the left.

Pass to the right of the first lake, then cross a stone bridge to pass the second lake on the left.

Keep going until you find a sleeper bridge over a ditch near a field boundary.

Over this bridge, follow way-marks on white-painted logs across the golf course to stile onto a lay-by on the A430.

Turn left in the lay-by to find a safe crossing of the main road. (Watch out for traffic turning into Park Road.) Continue along the pavement up Park Road to find a footpath along the drive of Ivory House on the left.

The path descends through the wood on to a metalled lane.

In the lane, turn right and continue across a new junction to the end of the lane.

It was at this junction that we found a group of benighted youths who gone exploring up the River Frome and had lost their way. We sent them to Badminton Road to find their way home to Downend.

The junction itself is an oddity. It seems to have something to do with maintenance work on the railway to the right.

At the end of the lane, turn left over the stile and descend to the river near the viaduct beside Huckford Quarry.

Huckford Quarry is maintained as a nature area. If you have time to visit it, turn right to find a bridge over the river and then left along the bank.

Turn left and follow the path along this attractive stretch of riverbank to a kissing gate onto a road.

You need to turn right here, which is a problem because you are on a blind bend. It is probably best to cross the road first, watching out for traffic from the right, cross Damson's Bridge and look for the side road on the left.

Follow the side road until the road swings right up hill. Go straight on, on a path to the left of a garage.

Follow the path to a footbridge across the river.

This is another attractive stretch of river and kingfishers have a perch beside the rapids to the right of the bridge.

Over the bridge turn right and follow the track through two kissing gates to a road.

Turn left and look for a footpath by three stakes on the left.

Follow this path uphill, up some steps and past a house to a stone stile into a field.

Make for the stone stile in the diagonally opposite corner of this field, *which is surrounded by the earthen remains of an Iron Age hill fort, called Bury Hill.*

FROM BURY HILL TO THE LANGLEY ARMS

Over the stile, turn right and right again to a crossroads.

Turn left down Church Lane and cross bridges over the motorway and the ring road.

Cross the ring road cycle path as well and then turn right down a cinder bridle path to a kissing-gate on the left beside an interpretive panel, which explains what you may see in the Conservation area.

Follow the path along Leap Valley to Badminton Road.

Cross the road to find a path along the next section of the stream which formed the Leap Valley.

When you reach an outpost of the City of Bristol College, pass it on your left and keep going to Beaufort Road.

Over Beaufort Road, follow the path to the left of the stream up to the main road. *Strangely enough, I once saw a kingfisher in this unlikely stream, which shows that you should keep your eyes open at all times, if you want to get the best out of nature.*

In the road turn left and then right up Elm Road beside the Hunters' Inn. Keep to the right of the green up to Blackhorse Road.

Cross over the road into Dibden Lane, which retains some rural charm, and follow it past Vinney Green Farm House back to emerge in Guest Avenue opposite the Langley Arms.

Go down the lane to the right of the pub, past the end of a green lane to a cycle trap bedside a gate.

Through the trap, turn right along the hedge, which hides the green lane, until the path goes up a steep bank.

Turn left along the top of the bank to a metalled path.

Turn right and then left between two playgrounds (one for toddlers and the other for larger children.) to a laurel circle.

Turn left to a path that descends to the right to emerge next to the Leapfrog Day Nursery.

Go straight ahead toward Botteloni's and the cross the road onto the path between Botteloni's (on the right) and the Mill House (on the left).

You will emerge in the car park near Boots. If you have come by bus, the bus stop is near Sainsbury on the right. If you came by car, I hope you remember where you left it!

8: 'MADE FOREVER!' OR 'THE WHISTLER' 7M

From Kingswood Heritage Museum, Tower Lane, Warmley

This jolly fellow is one of the miners who thought they were 'made forever' when a new coal seam was discovered nearby. This notable seam leant its name to the pub on the corner of Anchor Road and New Cheltenham Road called 'The Anchor, Made Forever'. There is also a chapel in Anchor Road whose name refers to the same event. It had originally been my

intention to start this route from the Anchor; but unfortunately, the drawing of Fisher Road from the Anchor to Siston Common gave the route map an appearance that might easily give offence, especially in a Wesleyan Methodist chapel!

Consequently, this route starts from the historical industrial centre of Warmley, namely the remains of William Campion's Brass Works, instead. William Campion was one of the many Quaker entrepreneurs who made their mark on eighteenth century England. Campion's works made use of the local coal and ore from the Mendips to make his brass. Two important parts of his works remain, The Clocktower building in Tower Road North and the Kingswood Heritage Museum in Tower Lane. Campion lived above the shop, as it were. His house is now a nursing home in Tower Road North but his garden complete with grottoes, which occupies the area behind the buildings, is open to the public.

The Museum, run by volunteers, is open every Tuesday from 2pm to 5pm. It is also open from 2 to 5 every Sunday from May to September (every second Sunday for the rest of the year) and Bank Holidays. It is a community museum in every sense, and the only museum near Bristol to acknowledge the City's mining traditions. It is the ideal place from which to explore the Kingswood and Parkfield Coalfields connecting the old coalmining communities of Kingswood and Mangotsfield.

However, the limited opening times also apply to the museum car park. So, if you wish to complete the route when the museum is shut, you may have to park round the corner at the Clocktower, or, at the weekend, in St Ivel Road. The 43 and 43A and the 319 bus all stop in Tower Road North. (Ask for St Ivel Way.)

Refreshments are available at the Museum when it is open, and there are several pubs en route, including the Anchor, the Horseshoe, the Langley Arms and the Midland Spinner.

FROM THE KINGSWOOD HERITAGE MUSEUM TO THE LANGLEY ARMS

From the Museum, turn right and right again down a made up path alongside the Siston Brook.

Follow the path until it emerges beside The Grange Community School.

Carry on past the school on the footpath alongside the Brook.

Follow the path until it emerges in a side road.

Turn right and follow it up to the main road.

Turn left to the pedestrian crossing and turn left again at the other side of the road.

Turn right into the cycle path along the right hand side of the ring road.

Keep to the lower (right hand track) until you cross the Siston Brook.

Turn left under the Ring Road and follow the cycle path as it dips under a tunnel onto the northern part of Siston Common.

A disused mine shaft is associated with Sistonhill Farm to the right of the cycle track.

After the cycle track crosses Warmley Brook and rounds a bend to the right, look for a tunnel off to the left. This leads to some steps up onto Rodway Hill Common.

At the top of the steps, go slightly left of straight on across the common towards Mangotsfield School.

Cross the road towards the school by the pedestrian crossing and then turn left and look for a gate into a field on the right.

Through the gate, turn left alongside a wall to the corner of the field.

Turn right and continue with a wall and houses on your left until you emerge on a road beside a sports ground.

Go straight across the road and up a back alley to the right of a car workshop in Elmleigh Road, which emerges in Colliers Break.

Go straight across Colliers Break and follow the path past a preserved slagheap and engine house to a path at the far end of the square.

The slagheap and engine house are two of the few pieces of industrial archaeology, associated with mining, that are readily accessible in the district.

The path emerges into Church Farm Road next to

Mangotsfield C of E Primary School. Go straight across and then left into Emerson's Green Lane.

When the road bends to the left, go straight ahead across the green, along side the backs of some houses.

Cross another road (confusingly also called Emerson's Green Lane) into another green space (Emerson's Green).

Look for delightfully preserved, muddy, green lane, slightly to the left and follow it until you reach the end on a tarmac road.

At end of lane, turn left if you are visiting The Langley Arms.

FROM THE LANGLEY ARMS TO LYDE GREEN

From the Langley Arms turn left and return to the end of the Green Lane. (If you have not visited the pub, you will turn right at this point!)

Go straight around a bend to the left to find a cycle path off to the right.

Following signs to the Ring Road cycle track; go along the cycle path to Adderley Gate (a road).

Cross this road and another, and then follow the cycle path between some houses to the Ring Road cycle path.

Turn right on the cycle path, then left over a footbridge. Keep going straight on down some steps to a stile on the far side of bridge.

Carry on with a hedge on your right through a gap to another stile.

Over this stile, carry on up the hill passing Hallen Farm on the right onto a drive.

Turn left on the drive and follow it to Howsmoor Lane.

Turn right and follow the lane through a green space.

As the lane bends to the left, go straight ahead down a green path until it crosses a boggy area by means of a sleeper bridge.

Over the bridge, follow the left hand hedge of some rough grazing. Keep going over a ditch as path swings to the right to emerge on the road near Lyde Green Farm.

THE FOREST PATH FROM LYDE GREEN TO THE KINGSWOOD HERITAGE MUSEUM

Bear left across the road to a kissing gate into a horse field.

In the field, keep the hedge on your left to find another kissing gate onto a disused railway path.

On the path, turn right.

When the path splits at a disused colliery, take the left fork and look for a kissing gate on the left just past the colliery stack.

Go through the gate to stile. (There is a gap beside it.)

Go straight ahead up a grassy track beside the quarry on your right.

At the top corner, turn right to a gateway on your left.

Through the gateway, go straight on up with a hedge on your left to a stile.

Keep going on up to an iron gate.

Squeeze through the gap to the left of the gate onto a drive and follow the drive onto a road.

Go straight on uphill and round one bend to the right.

Just before the second bend, look for a kissing gate on the left.

In the field, go straight on along a tractor track, past a hedge corner to a gap in the hedge and a tall kissing-gate in a deer fence beyond.

Through the fence bear right down through the trees to another tall kissing gate and a wicket gate onto a major road. (This can be a struggle at the end of the summer when the path can get very overgrown.)

Cross the road and turn right along the verge to find a stile into the field on the left.

In the field, bear right to a gate in the bottom right hand corner.

Through the gate, go straight-ahead, keeping a hedge on your right to a stile.

Over the stile, go straight ahead across a large field to find a kissing gate just below the middle of the opposite hedge.

In the next field, bear right to the lowest gap beside the golf course in the diagonally opposite corner.

Through the gap, make for a gate in the opposite side of a triangular field.

Through the gate, bear slightly left of a wooden electricity pole across the field to a kissing gate thirty metres from the field corner.

This stile is on the line of a roman road.

In the next field, go straight-ahead, keeping the hedge on your right. (Look out for horse fences.)

Go through two kissing gates on either side of a track. In the next field, follow the left hand hedge to a redundant kissing gate in the corner.

Go round the kissing gate and another gate and follow a nettly track up to a gate into a tarmac drive.

Go straight up the drive to the road at Goose Green.

Cross Goose Green Road and turn left and immediately right down a drive to a kissing gate.

In the field, carry straight on to find a kissing gate on your right.

Through the gate, turn left and then right through another kissing gate.

Turn right and follow the right hand hedge past a gap.

Keep right when the path forks and carry on down to the end.

Turn right to a stile by a hedge (there is also a gap).

Go straight on, bearing slightly right of some trees, with some houses on your right, across a drive and down to a road.

Turn sharp left beside a signpost onto the Dramway, under an arch and down to a stile onto London Road.

Cross the road by the pedestrian crossing and turn left to find the Dramway Path on the left, just before the Midland Spinner.

When the path clears the warehouse on the right, look for a path, sloping up beside the garages on the left, which leads into a graveyard.

Follow the path to the church porch and turn right to a gate onto a lane.

Turn right and follow the path over the Dramway and the Railway Cycle path into an enclosed path between some industrial buildings.

In St Ivel Road, turn right to Tower Road North.

Turn left and cross the road to the Clock Tower.

Turn left and follow the road round to the right to get back the Kingswood Heritage Museum.

9: COCKRIDGE
OR 'THE CREATURE FROM THE DEEP' 9M
From Kingswood Heritage Museum, Tower Lane, Warmley

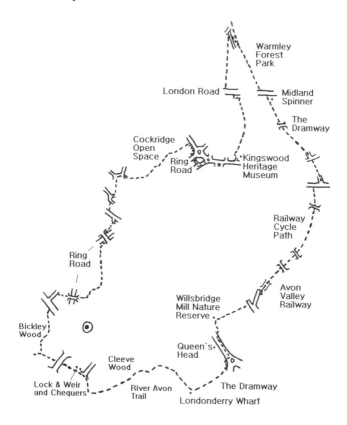

This map of the second excursion from the Kingswood Heritage Museum resembles a dugong or a manatee. Both of these are strange mammals, which inhabit shallow seas and rivers. This one is clearly using the slope of the Dramway to escape into the River Avon, where like the coal barges of old, it can make its way down river to Bristol and the sea.

The museum is run by volunteers, so it is only open on Tuesday afternoons and Sunday afternoons during the summer. On the other hand, there is a tearoom there, when it is open, and they offer guided tours of the nearby grottoes on Bank Holidays. It is the only museum in the area, which takes any notice of the coalfield. It houses a coalmining exhibit, as well as exhibits relating to local industries and other matters of local concern.

This section of the Forest Path also offers an opportunity to explore the Dramway Path from Siston Common, through a wooded cutting, along a section of the Railway Path, through the Willsbridge Valley Nature Reserve and through some paddocks to the Londonderry Wharf on the River Avon. The riverbank from Londonderry Wharf to Hanham Mills has Cleve Wood on one side and views across the meadows to the Cadbury Works and Keynsham Church on the other.

The return from Hanham Mills adds a climb through Bickley Woods on the banks of the River Avon, new planting at Hanham Green, a little thicket and views of the South Cotswolds in the fields outside the ring road and more views and thickets on Cock Ridge.

There is a car park at the Heritage Museum in Tower Lane Warmley, when it is open, and another at the Clock Tower, round the Corner in Tower Road North. The 43, 43A and 310 buses stop close to the Heritage Museum in Tower Road North. (Ask for St Ivel Road, where it is also convenient to park, especially at the weekend.)

Refreshments are available at the museum when it is open and the Midland Spinner in Warmley, at the Mill and the Queen's Head in Willsbridge, at the Chequers and the Lockand Weir in Hanham Mills and at The Elm Tree on Abbot's Road.

FROM THE HERITAGE MUSEUM TO SISTON COMMON

Between the museum and the car park, turn left into the Kingsway Trailer Park.

You will notice that nearly all the trailers have taken root and acquired tiled roofs and other attributes of permanent dwellings, which, of course, they are not!

Make your way towards the Statue of Neptune at the far end of the Trailer Park.

Neptune's Statue is one of the features of the garden of Warmley Court, now a nursing home. The Statue used to stand at the end of a large lake that covered the Trailer Park. If you have time, the garden is well worth an exploration. However, it is better to go there when the grottoes are open to the public.

Beside the statue, look for a path onto a track on the right.

On the track*, turn left alongside the remains of the leat, which used to carry water to the Echo Pond, in the gardens.

*If you want to visit the gardens, turn right and then return to this point.

Follow the path until it emerges on the road leading to The Grange Community School.

Turn left toward the school and then right on the footpath alongside the Siston Brook.

Follow the path until it emerges in a side road.

Turn right and follow up to the main road.

Turn left to the pedestrian crossing and turn left again at the other side of the road.

Turn right into the cycle path along the right hand side of the Ring Road.

Keep to the lower (right hand track) until you cross the Siston Brook. .

Over Siston Brook go straight ahead up the track, which leads up to the cycle track.

Keep on the track past a cattle grid.

Then turn left and then right onto the Dramway Path.

FROM SISTON COMMON TO LONDONDERRY WHARF

When you come out onto the London Road, cross over by the pedestrian crossing and turn down the path between the Midland Spinner and a warehouse.

Continue on the path under an arch, across Grasmere Gardens, along Windermere Way, across Poplar Road to emerge past some warehouses in Southway Drive.

Turn right and then left down the Bristol and Bath Railway Path. Continue past Oldland Station and under three bridges.

Just after the railway path goes <u>over</u> a bridge, turn right into a residential street.

Follow the street to T-junction and then look for a kissing gate ahead into the Willsbridge Valley Nature Reserve.

Follow the path past the bottom of the California Incline through a gate to Willsbridge Mill.

The California incline brought coal to the Dramway from the California pit, which was optimistically named after the California Gold Rush.

At the Mill, continue alongside the stream through the 'ecological' garden to emerge opposite the Queen's Head.

The Forest Path goes through the pub car park and along the Siston Brook to the River Avon at Londonderry Wharf. However, this part of the Path is poorly maintained and can be deeply rutted and overgrown with brambles, so in spite of the fact that I once saw a kingfisher flashing down the brook ahead of me, I prefer to follow the Dramway at this point. This route also has the advantage of suiting the theme of this route rather better.

Turn left and follow the pavement up to the roundabout.

Cross the road carefully and turn left and then right down the road to Keynsham.

Look for a stile into the field on your right.

Over the stile, turn left and the bed of the Dramway until you reach a stile.

At this point there used to be a junction in the Dramway. The original course turned left through the tunnel that you can just make out under the road to Keynsham. It terminated on the riverbank opposite the Broadmead Lane Industrial Estate. The branch down to Londonderry Wharf was built to avoid paying for barges to use the Keynsham Lock on the way to Bristol.

Go over the stile and a kissing gate on the other side of the drive.

Follow the path through the field to a pair of kissing gates beside a cottage.

Carry on to the riverbank and turn right.

This is Londonderry Wharf.

FROM LONDONDERRY WHARF TO HANHAM MILLS

Keep going along the riverbank toward Hanham Mills.

There is a right of way along the tow path all the way, but you may prefer to take a short cut in the fourth and last field by following the line of the electricity pylons.

On a sunny day the views across the river toward Keynsham church and the old Fry's Chocolate Factory and it is worth keeping an eye out for kestrels hunting along the wood side.

You approach Hanham Mills beside the car park of the Chequers Inn, which stands on the corner of Ferry Road. However, the second pub along the river, The Lock and Weir, is generally more highly rated by real ale drinkers.

FROM HANHAM MILLS TO KINGSWOOD HERITAGE MUSEUM

Carry on down river past the Lock and Weir. **(The actual weir is on your left, although it can be hard to see if the water is very high.)**

When the track forks, bear right along the higher track under the ring road. (Ignore footpaths off to the right just before and just after the bridge.)

About two hundred and forty metres past the bridge turn right up signed path into the wood.

This is Bickley Wood, part of the Avon Valley Woodlands Nature Reserve.

Follow the path up through wood (The trail has been complicated by adventurous mountain bikers, but if you keep going uphill, slightly right of straight on, you shouldn't go far wrong, provided you take account of the quarries!)

After about three hundred metres, the path goes up a concrete path beside a stream.

After another couple of hundred metres or so you should emerge by a pub on Abbots Road called the Elm Tree.

In the road, turn left and then right up Crossleaze Road.

At end of road, go through a kissing gate by 'The Old Barn' and turn right through another kissing gate into a field.

Note the new planting in the field between the kissing gates.
Follow the left hand hedge to a stile, which leads to a footbridge over the Ring Road.

On the other side, go through a kissing gate and then over a stile into a field.

Ignore the wooden stile on the left and go straight ahead to a stone stile into another field.

Follow the left hand hedge uphill to a kissing gate into a muddy little wood on the left.

Go up through wood to another kissing gate into a field.

Follow the right hand hedge to a metal stile with a stone step.

There are extensive views of the South Cotswolds from here. You should be able to make out the clump of trees on the conical summit of Kelston Round Hill and a line of beeches on the horizon on Freezing Hill.

Over the stile, bear left past a trig point to a double stile.

Over this stile, bear right down hill to a stile in the corner with a wicket gate beyond it.

Through the gate, bear right to a stile with a new kissing gate beyond it on the other side of a track.

Follow the path alongside the Ring Road to the road ahead.

Turn left and then right at the pedestrian lights.

Follow the path on the left side of the Ring Road.

Take the first turning on the left and then turn right in the street.

Follow the tarmac path ahead (or cut across the grass) into another cul-de-sac and continue to a T-junction.

Turn left and then right into Greenbank Playing Field.

In the field, follow the right hand hedge to emerge in Kingsfield Lane.

In the road, go straight ahead and then first right into a lane.

Turn immediately left to a pinch stile next to iron gates leading to Kingsfield Farm.

Follow a path between hedges to another pinch stile into a road.

In this road, take the first track on the right, which leads to a cycle trap into Cockridge Open Space.

There used to be several mines around Cock Road. It is possibly the risk of subsidence that has left the open space undeveloped.

There are several paths through the open space, but the views are best from higher up, so try to follow the top boundary of the field.

After you have been forced to descend, bear left uphill past an oak tree to the top hedge.

Descend some steps and then go left and up again.

Leave the open space down a slope into the road at the far end.

In Wraxall Road, turn right and descend to the subway under the ring road.

Through the tunnel, go straight ahead down the cycle path to Craven Way and turn left to a mini roundabout. Cross over and turn right along Tower Lane and look for the Kingswood Heritage Museum on the left.

10: TWO RIVERS
OR LION/FISH 20M, 14M or 13M
From Eastville Park car park, Park Avenue, Eastville

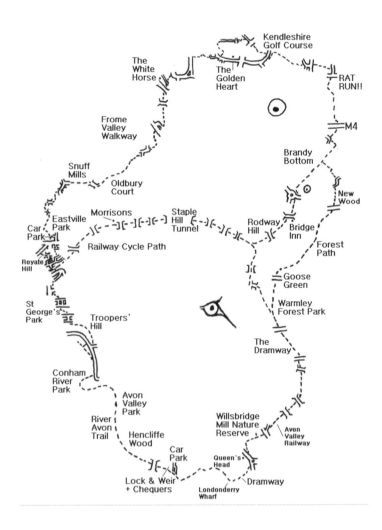

Kendleshire
Golf Course

The
White
Horse

The
Golden
Heart

RAT
RUN!!

Frome
Valley
Walkway

M4

Brandy
Bottom

Snuff
Mills

New
Wood

Oldbury
Court

Morrisons

Staple
Hill
Tunnel

Rodway
Hill

Bridge
Inn

Eastville
Park

Car
Park

Railway Cycle Path

Forest
Path

Royate
Hill

Goose
Green

St
George's
Park

Warmley
Forest Park

Troopers'
Hill

The
Dramway

Conham
River
Park

Avon
Valley
Park

River
Avon
Trail

Willsbridge
Mill Nature
Reserve

Avon
Valley
Railway

Hencliffe
Wood

Car
Park

Queen's
Head

Lock & Weir
+ Chequers

Londonderry
Wharf

Dramway

This strange collection of creatures cannot quite decide whether it belongs in a menagerie, an aquarium or a freak show. This is not surprising, because, like the Patchway and Bradley Stoke route, this set of routes has been cobbled together from pre-existing published routes. This fulfils one of the original intentions of the Community Forest Path, which was to provide links between the linear routes which radiate out from the centre of Bristol. The Frome Walkway, the Avon River Trail and the Bristol and Bath Railway Cycle Path are all implicated in this farrago, as is the Dramway, which shadows the Forest Path through the fringes of the South Gloucestershire Coalfield.

It would have made sense to start these routes from Bristol Bridge, where the Frome Walkway and the Avon Trail meet, not far from the beginning of the Railway Cycle Path. This would have produced a route of literally marathon proportions, and those who are preparing to take on the full challenge of the Forest Path will probably get hold of the relevant leaflets and work it into their preparations. We have opted instead for a slightly more modest twenty-mile route originating from Eastville Park, which, like all of Bristol's parks, claims to be at the heart of the Forest of Avon. It has the additional advantage that the Railway Cycle Path divides it into two shorter routes of fourteen and thirteen miles, which are more manageable. The shorter of these is the southern one, in spite of the appearance of the sketch map. Both are also accessible from the car park of Morrison's supermarket in Fishponds, which is probably more secure than Eastville, but the twenty-mile route would not work from there. You will probably already spotted a much shorter route peeping out shyly between the other two, which can be accessed from the Bridge Inn at Shortwood.

Eastville Park car park is at the end of Park Avenue, a cul-de-sac off Oakdene Avenue, the turning off Fishponds Road past the shops on the way out of Bristol. Buses number 4, 28, 48 and 49 stop nearby.

Apart form the Queen's Head in Fishponds Road, opposite the entrance to the park, refreshments are available at The Midland

Spinner in Warmley, Willsbridge Mill and the Queen's Head in Willsbridge and the Lock and Weir and the Chequers at Hanham Mills. In addition, the White Horse at Hambrook and the Golden Heart are both accessible from the longer route, and there is often a snack wagon at the lay-by, where the Forest Path crosses the Badminton Road, and it is sometimes possible to visit the Half-Way café on the Kendleshire Golf Course.

FROM EASTVILLE PARK TO HAMBROOK

From the car park, turn right past the Eastville Park Community Garden and follow the path past until you can turn right again down the steps to Eastville Lake.

Turn right past the end of the lake to the track alongside the River Avon.

Follow the river upstream to a footbridge over the river past a weir.

Over the river, turn right across the grass to a track across Wickham Bridge back over the River Frome.

Over the river, turn left into a meadow and follow the river to emerge over a stile by some terraced houses.

By the houses, turn right up some steps. There is no right of way over the lower path.

At the top of the steps, turn left down Blackberry Hill toward the road bridge over the Frome.

Turn right down River View to Snuff Mills Park.

Follow the path alongside the river until you can turn right across a footbridge over the river.

Turn left and follow the riverbank to the end of Oldbury Court Estate (or Vassall's Park).

In the road, turn left over an old stone bridge. This is Frenchay Bridge, now closed to motor traffic.

Turn right.

After the road bends round to the left, turn right down Chapel Lane to a stone stile into a meadow.

Go straight ahead through meadow and look for a kissing gate into the access land on the right (Frenchay Moor, owned by the National Trust.)

Go uphill towards the diagonally opposite corner of the field. Just before the corner, go left through a gateway and then right to a kissing gate onto a road.

Cross the road and turn left across the grass to Grange Park. *The Tower on the grass is a dovecote, which used to belong to the original Grange Park.*

In the modern Grange Park, look for a turning off to the left and a gate to a track down to the river.

Continue to follow the Frome upstream until you pass under the second road bridge. (It's the M4.)

After you have gone under the motorway, go over a stile beside a gate into a road and follow it round to the left, past two footpaths joining from the left, across the bridge over the Bradley Brook - a river at this point- to the footpath through a gap beside a single rail on the right.

THE FOREST PATH FROM HAMBROOK TO BRANDY BOTTOM COLLIERY

If you are walking, this is a good spot to decide where you are going to stop for refreshment. The White Horse is up the lane to the left. (There are a couple of other pubs in Hambrook, but I have not tried them yet.) The Golden Heart in Kendleshire is closer to half way round, but visiting it means using rather more of a diversion from the Forest Path on the road than some may think proper!

If you are training for a marathon, it's better not to think about it! Just take a swig from your water bottle and carry on!

Follow the path alongside the River Frome on your right.

At the end of the path, turn right on the road across the river. Take care as there is a blind bend.

Go straight on at the first junction.

At the next junction there is a route choice. The shorter option is to turn left, following the Frome Walkway signs, which keeps you closer to the river. The Community Forest signs take you straight on up the hill, across one crossroad and then left down a track; turn left over a stile on your left and follow the path to a stone stile in the diagonally opposite corner of the hill fort and then make your way down a steep path (involving steps) to the road.

In either case, turn right alongside the river just before the road crosses a bridge.

Follow the track through a new kissing gate and an older one until you reach a footbridge over the river.

Over the river turn right along a substantial path, which emerges past a garage into 'The Dingle'.

Go straight ahead to a T-junction and then turn right over the river.

Turn left through a kissing gate on the other side and follow the enclosed path alongside the river.

The Forest Path veers off to the right just before the first stile to block the path close to a railway viaduct. Do not climb the stile but turn right to a stile into a lane up the hill.

Follow the lane over a new crossroad, and turn left into a wood.

In the wood, bear right.

The correct trail is the furthest right of three, but it is not the end of the world if you go up the most obvious track, you just end up a little further up Park Lane.

In any case, on the road, turn right to a T-junction.

This major road is the A432 or Badminton Road, but there is good visibility in both directions so you should have no trouble crossing to a kissing gate in the lay-by opposite into Kendleshire Golf Course

In the golf course, go straight across the fairway following route markers in the form of sawn off stumps on telegraph poles, painted white.

Go left of one pond, over a plank and right of the next pond. Cross a stone bridge on the left before the pond and continue on the left hand side of that pond onto a cinder track.

Turn right to a kissing gate onto a road. You are supposed to turn right on the road and then left at kissing gate onto the golf course.

On the golf course keep left alongside hedge.

You need to cross a wooden bridge back to the gate opposite the kissing gate where you left the first part of the golf course. In any case, you need to keep alongside the hedge on the left, ignoring any tracks or paths until you get to a corner next to a field gate.

Turn right on another cinder track and then left past a shack or café.

Keep on the track until you enter the car park behind the clubhouse.

In the car park, bear left onto the exit drive, and then, when the drive turns to the left go straight on across the grass to a kissing gate onto the road.

Cross the road and turn right along the pavement to a junction on the left.

Turn left toward Bitterwell Lake and then right through a kissing gate onto the Dramway Path.

Go straight ahead through one makeshift gate, a kissing gate and a horse gate that leads past a house onto a road.

In the road, turn right to Westerleigh Road. This road provides a short cut from junction 18 on the M4 so the traffic on it is faster and more frequent than you might expect, so take care!

Cross this road to gap beside a field gate into a bridle path.

Follow the bridle path to a kissing gate and a signpost on the left just past a horse walking device in the farmyard on the left.

In the field, bear right to a barb-wired field gate in the diagonally opposite corner. *(The scrubby bump in the middle of field is a disused mineshaft.)*

Over the wire, go straight ahead with a hedge on your left to a gateway.

Keep going straight on to a double stile and bridge.

Go straight ahead to a kissing gate and then bear left to find a tunnel under the motorway (M4). (Take care! One of the gates has an unexpected shin-catcher.)

Through the tunnel, go straight ahead past Lyde Green Farm onto a road.

On the road, turn left through a kissing gate into a horse field.

Turn left along the hedge to find a kissing gate onto a branch off the railway path.

Turn right.

Carry straight on when the railway path goes over road.

Take the left hand fork, when the path splits at a disused colliery (Brandy Bottom Colliery), and look for a kissing gate on the left.

FROM BRANDY BOTTOM TO EASTVILLE PARK

Go straight ahead down the cycle over one cross road until you reach a junction just before the Ring Road.

Bear left to find a tunnel under the road.

On the other side bear right alongside the ring road until you reach some steps up on the left, which emerge opposite the Bridge Inn at Shortwood.

This is an excellent community pub, which serves rough cider and good beer.

From the pub, cross over the ring road and turn right and right again onto the cycle path along the other side of the ring road.

At this point, we leave the Dramway.

Follow the path through the old Mangotsfield Railway Station at the bottom of Rodway Common and keep going until Staple Hill Railway Tunnel.

From the tunnel, count four overhead road bridges and then right off the cycle track beside an upside down brick fish to Morrisons.

For Eastville Park, carry on under two more bridges, and turn right into a cul-de-sac just before the railway path goes over a bridge.

Turn left and right between some flats and round to a green, from which you will find some steps up onto the Royate Hill Viaduct , now a Local Nature Reserve.

Over the Viaduct, turn right along the road that emerges below the Queen's Head opposite Eastville Park.

FROM BRANDY BOTTOM TO LONDON ROAD

Through the kissing gate, go straight ahead to a stile (There is a gap next to it.) and follow the enclosed path around the corner of the quarry to an open gate or gap on the left.

Go up through a scrubby wood to a stile and then follow the path past a house to a gap beside a gate onto a drive.

Follow drive up to a road.

Go straight on up the hill and round one bend.

Just before the second bend, look for a kissing gate on the left.

Go straight across the field along a tractor track, past a hedge corner to a gap in the corner of the field.

Go through the gap and a tall kissing-gate in a deer fence.

Bear right through a new plantation to another deer gate and another gate onto a major road.

Cross the road and turn right along the pavement to find a stile into the field on the left.

In the field, bear right to a gate in the bottom right hand corner.

Go straight-ahead, keeping hedge on right to another stile.

Over the stile, go straight ahead across a large field to find a kissing gate just below middle of opposite hedge.

Bear right to a gap in diagonally opposite corner of the field.

Through the gap (the lower of the two) make for a gate in the opposite side of the triangular field.

Bear slightly left across the next field to a kissing gate fifty metres up from the corner of the field.

Go straight-ahead, through the horse paddocks looking out for electric horse fencing and gates.

Go over two kissing gates on either side of a track.

In next field, follow the left hand hedge to a gate in the corner.

Follow the nettly track up to a stile onto a tarmac drive.

Go straight up the drive to Goose Green.

Turn left and then right up a drive to a kissing gate into a field.

In the field, carry straight on to find a kissing gate on your right.

Through the gate, turn left and then right through another kissing gate.

Turn right and follow the right hand hedge past a gap.

Keep right when the path forks and carry on down to the end.

Turn right to a stile by a hedge (there is also a gap).

Go straight on, bearing slightly right of some trees, with some houses on your right, across a drive and down to a road. Turn sharp left beside a signpost onto the Dramway and follow it under an arch and down to a stile onto London Road, where the twenty-mile route joins the southern route from Eastville Park

FROM EASTVILLE PARK TO LONDON ROAD

From the car park, go up Park Avenue to Oakdene Avenue and turn right.

Cross Fishponds Road and turn right to find Shamrock Road on your left.

At the end of the road, turn right and look for a footpath on your left. At the bottom the path, turn left and then right to find some steps up to a road.

Carry on up the hill and turn left into Clay Bottom.

Keep going until you find a gap onto the cycle path on your right.

Turn right along the Bristol and Bath Railway Cycle Path and keep going for about 4 miles until you rejoin the main route at the London Road in Warmley.

FROM LONDON ROAD TO HANHAM MILLS

Cross the London Road by the pedestrian crossing and turn left to find the Dramway Path as it disappears between a warehouse and the Midland Spinner public house on the right.

Continue on the path under an arch, across Grasmere gardens, along Windermere way, across Poplar Road to emerge past some warehouses in Southway Drive.

Turn right and then left down the Bristol and Bath Railway Cycle Path.

Continue along the B&B path until about half a kilometre past Oldland Common Railway station, where the Bitton Railway starts.

After the railway path goes **over** a road, turn right and then left up a path into a road called Cherry Wood.

At the end of the road turn right and immediately left through a kissing gate into Willsbridge Valley Nature Reserve.

Go straight ahead past the bottom of the California Incline and over a stile to Willsbridge Mill and then through the ecological garden to the road opposite the Queen's Arms.

Turn left and then right into the Queen's Arms' car park and follow the path alongside the stream to Londonderry Wharf on the River Avon.

At the Wharf, turn right to follow the towpath to Hanham Mills.

There is a right of way along the tow path all the way, but you may prefer to take a short cut in the fourth and last field by following the line of the electricity pylons.

You approach Hanham Mills beside the car park of the Chequers Inn, which stands on the corner of Ferry Road. However, the second pub along the river, The Lock and Weir, is generally more highly rated by real ale drinkers.

FROM HANHAM MILLS TO CLAY BOTTOM

Keep going past the Lock and Weir and follow the Monarch's Way /Towing Path alongside the River Avon for about two miles past the car park at Conham River Park to emerge on Conham Road, where you must turn left. (The pavement is on far side of the road.)

Continue along the pavement until you can see footpath on the opposite side of road.

Follow footpath downstream on riverbank, beside some new houses and look for a footpath between the houses back to the road.

On the road, turn right and then left up Troopers Hill Road and look for the access to the Troopers Hill nature Reserve on the left, just past the stack of Troopers Hill (disused) Colliery.

In the open space, take the path that goes left before turning uphill to another disused chimney.

Troopers Hill is a Local Nature Reserve. It is described in the Website of the Friends of Troopers Hill at www.troopers-hill.org.uk. The Friends recently received a lottery grant (October 2006) to produce a set of three leaflets describing the site. But the website contains most of the information you might require in any case, including a map, history and wildlife description.

You will probably want to go up to the chimney, which commands some magnificent views, but the path you need branches off to the left before you reach it. From the chimney, it is better to continue uphill to a dog bin before descending to intercept the path into the Crews Hole Woodland Walk.

Keep going as close to straight ahead as you can to emerge on Beaufort Road.

Seek out Beaconsfield Road, which is the next on the right.

Follow Beaconsfield Road up to the main road.

Cross main the road to enter St George's Park by the path alongside the library.

In the park, descend to the left of the lake and ascend the other side to a road.

Go straight ahead up Congleton Road to another main road (Whitehall Road).

Over this road, turn right and then left up Thurstan's Barton to find a cinder track behind the houses to Gordon Avenue.

Turn left to the main road, and then right.

Take the track to the right past some playing fields into a cul-de-sac.

Follow the cul-de-sac to a main road.

Turn left and look for a path onto the Railway Cycle Path on the right.

On the Cycle Path, turn left and then right into a cul-de-sac.

At the junction with Clay Bottom, turn left and then right down Wainbrook Drive and right again up Crabtree Walk.

Across the grass, look for a gap to some steps leading up the railway embankment.

Turn left along the top of the viaduct over Royate Hill.

This is the Royate Hill Nature Reserve, which is managed by Bristol Parks and Avon Wildlife Trust. It was saved from the developers following a vigorous campaign in 1996, when it was compulsorily purchased in what must have been one of the last acts of Avon County Council. There are good views from the top over Greenbank Cemetery on the left as well as towards Eastville park on the right.

At end of the reserve, turn right down Edward Street to emerge at the top of Royate Hill, just below the Queen's Head.

Turn left and cross Fishponds Road into Eastville Park by the traffic lights and turn right on the peripheral path to emerge at the beginning of the Sri Chinmoy Peace Mile beside the car park.

11: CHEW VALLEY
AND CHARLTON PLATEAU
OR 'THE TWO QUEENS' 15M
From Bath Hill car park, Keynsham

(Rising Sun and George and Dragon)

This peculiar pair has taken its form from the map of a couple of conjoined routes - one from Keynsham to Compton Dando and returning via Woollard and Queen Charlton - and the other from Whitchurch to Compton Dando and Pensford via Chewton Keynsham and Norton Malreward.

I have written it up as a single 15-mile route, because I like to avoid roads. As it stands, this route illustrates the opposite principle to that of 'The Other Avon Gorge'. That is, it is often possible to divide a long route up into shorter chunks to suit your ability and the time that you have available to you.

The description starts from the car park in Keynsham, but there is also a railway station in Keynsham and it is served by buses no. 178, 318, 349, 532, 533 and 636.

There are dozens of places where refreshments are available in Keynsham and you could stop en route at The Compton Inn, the George and Dragon and the Rising Sun in Pensford and at the Maes Knoll and Horse World in Whitchurch.

FROM KEYNSHAM TO THE COMPTON INN

From the Bath Hill long-stay car park, cross the River Chew by means of the wooden footbridge and turn left.

Follow the river upstream, as closely as you can (for about half a mile) until you emerge in a cul-de-sac.

At the junction turn right and then left.

Turn left again where the path goes through an old people's home to the riverside.

Follow the river as closely as you can until it emerges through a kissing gate onto a road on a blind corner.

Go straight ahead down the road and then left through a kissing gate into a field.

In the field, go over a small bridge and follow the river to a double-gate into another field.

In the field go straight ahead to a kissing gate onto a track.

Cross the track to a kissing gate opposite.

Through the kissing gate, follow the riverbank to a bridge and stile.

Over the stile, follow the riverbank to a kissing gate.

Through the kissing gate, bear right to a kissing gate on the horizon.

Through this gate, turn left to a bridge and another kissing gate.

Through the gate follow the track alongside a grassy bank (cowslips in spring) to a kissing gate into a wood.

At end of the wood, go straight ahead to a kissing gate at end of field beside the river.

Through the gate, follow the riverbank to another kissing gate.

Through this kissing gate, the path shadows the line of the right hand hedge to a kissing gate onto the road.

On the road, turn left over a bridge to **The Compton Inn.**

FROM THE COMPTON INN TO PENSFORD

From the Compton Inn, go up the road to the church opposite. Follow the path through the churchyard, down some steps into a stable yard.

In the yard, bear right around the buildings to a gate.

Through the gate, go straight ahead through the paddocks to a footbridge over the Chew.

Over the bridge, bear left to a stile into a wood.

Follow the path up through the wood to a kissing gate into a field. *There are several fallen trees over the path through the wood.*

In the field, go straight ahead to a kissing gate.

In the next field, go straight ahead through a gate and then on to a kissing gate at the top of a steep descent.

Make your way carefully down the path, which has the character of a cattle path at this point and make your forward to a field gate onto a metalled track.

On the track, go straight ahead to emerge on a tarmac lane in Woollard.

In Woollard, turn left and left again over the bridge across the Chew.

Over the bridge, turn right to a footbridge to the right of a RUPP and bear right across the field to a stile near the riverbank.

The RUPP follows a streambed that is part of the course of the Compton Dandy Run, an off-road running race put on by Town and Country Harriers during one evening in the summer, usually on August.

Over the stile, go straight ahead to a gate onto a track.

Carry straight on along the farm track to a bridge over the River Chew.

Over the bridge, go straight ahead along the field, past the church and along the riverbank to a kissing-gate onto the road.

In the road, turn left and cross the bridge to a kissing-gate on the left.

In the field, bear right to another kissing-gate.

Through the gate, bear right to a kissing-gate onto the road.

In the road, turn left and go down to the road junction near the famous lockup for rowdy miners.

If you are looking for refreshments, the George and Dragon is up to the left, and the Rising Sun is the other side of the main road.

FROM PENSFORD TO NORTON MALREWARD

From the lockup, go down to the main A37 and turn right to find a pedestrian crossing.

When you have crossed the road, turn right and then left at the first junction.

Just before the Rising Sun, turn right up a track.

When track the divides, fork left under the viaduct to a kissing gate.

Keep left along side the wood to kissing gate on the left into a field.

In the field, follow the river upstream through two more kissing gates.

After the second kissing gate, bear right to a kissing gate in the middle of a hedge on the right.

Continue uphill with the hedge on your right to a kissing gate in the top right corner of the field.

Through the gate, go straight ahead to kissing gate on the left onto a road. (CAUTION B3130!)

On the road, turn left and first right up a stony track.

Go straight up the track to emerge in a field.

Go straight ahead on the track across the field, over the brow of the hill and across a grass landing strip. CAUTION it is used!

As the track turns left alongside a fence, look for a path on the right through some converted farm buildings.

Follow the right of way between the conversions onto the drive to the church and then turn right down to the main street of Norton Malreward.

FROM NORTON MALREWARD TO HORSEWORLD

Turn right again and look for a kissing gate on the right, as the road bends to the left.

Through the gate, the official right of way goes diagonally across an arable field, but there is an obviously preferable track around the right hand edge of the field to a double stile over a bridge in the diagonally opposite corner. (The first stile was destroyed the last time I saw it.)

Over the stile, go slightly left of straight ahead to another stile*, and continue on the same line to a kissing gate onto a minor road.

*The Wansdyke is supposed to run through the field before this stile, but it does not look convincing on the ground.

Turn left to find another kissing gate into the field opposite.

In the field, go along length of field to a pair of horse gates below Whitewood Farm and then go straight ahead to a kissing gate. (The narrow field on the right is a disused railway.)

In the next field, as the disused railway peels away to the right, the right of way heads for the gates in the diagonally opposite corner of the field. However, the laying of a pipeline interrupted this route in 2005/6 and the path was diverted around the right hand edge of the field. The path has not been restored to its original path at the time of going to press.

In the far corner, take the right hand wicket gate beside a muddy field gate.

In the next field, go straight ahead to a stile.

Over the stile, go straight ahead, with a hedge on your left and then through a gateway to carry on in the same direction with the hedge on your right.

Over a stile, descend to a stream crossing.

Over the stream, bear left through a hedge toward a church, and then right alongside the hedge to a kissing gate and path between the houses to Bristol Road, Whitchurch.

In the road, turn left and then right at the traffic lights beside the Maes Knoll public house.

Follow the road (Staunton Lane) for about 500m. It is safest to keep on left hand pavement as the road bends to the left to 'Horse World'.

FROM HORSEWORLD TO QUEEN CHARLTON

Turn right along the path under the trees alongside the drive (originally Staunton Lane), which is just past the entrance to the car park at Horseworld.

The path from here to Queen Charlton is essentially straight ahead for nearly 1500m. But there are some complications.

First, you must look out for a stile into the paddock on the left.

In the field, turn right and keep the fence on your right as the path goes over a stile to the right of a building.

When the path crosses a farm track look out for the stile into an enclosed path ahead.

Caution! The proposed route of the South Bristol Ring Road crosses the footpath at or near this point.

At the end of the enclosed track, over a stile, look for a gateway on the right.

Through the gateway, turn left to a stile and bridge over a stream at the bottom of the slope.

Over the bridge, go straight up through a new plantation to a kissing gate. (It is slightly to the left.)

Through the gate, go straight ahead, alongside the golf course on the left, through one gateway to emerge in a by-way (Engine House Lane).

Go straight ahead over a stile toward Queen Charlton Church.

In the field, follow the left hand hedge to a stile into an enclosed path ahead.

Follow the path over a stile to emerge on the green beside St Margaret's Church in Queen Charlton.

A plaque on the left, as you leave the path, says this is the Priest Path from Whitchurch, a phrase whose meaning is made clear by the ancient preaching cross on the green. Queen Charlton must have been part of Whitchurch at one time, and it would seem that St Margaret's began as a chapel of ease for the inhabitants of the village.

FROM QUEEN CHARLTON TO KEYNSHAM

Turn left down the lane at the other side of the green.

Follow the lane between some impressive looking houses and barn conversions until you reach a kissing gate into a field.

Bear left and then follow the path down to a stile onto a footbridge in the diagonally opposite corner.

There is an impressive new plantation on the hill opposite.

Over the bridge, turn left and follow the path alongside the left hand hedge to a stile into the field ahead.

Over this stile, go straight ahead on a path along the length of the field to a stile in the hedge ahead.

Over this stile, turn left and go straight ahead over a cross-path to find a stile in the bottom left hand corner of the field.

Over this stile, go straight ahead past a fishing lake and a field of vegetables to a stile and turn left.

Go straight on down to a badger sett and turn right alongside the stream to a stile into a paddock

Cross the paddock to a gate onto a gravel track between paddocks to a stile into a stable block.

Carry on through the buildings to a stile and gate into a car park.

At the other end, go through a small gate onto a path to the right of the stream to a bridge onto a road and turn right to the A4175 into Keynsham.

Cross the road and turn left onto a cobbled remnant of the old road past the soccer ground. (You may have to use the pedestrian bridge at some times of the day.)

Turn right through a kissing gate onto a path beside the stream.

Follow the path towards the Keynsham by-pass and turn right over a bridge across the stream.

Follow the path alongside the by-pass to a stile ahead into a path and then a road beside a terrace, which emerges on a major road next to Keynsham parish church.

The railway station is off to the left. If you need to wait for a train, there is a recently redecorated pub called the Pioneer to your right.

Cross straight across the road into Park Road and follow it into the park.

In the park, follow the path down the hill to the riverside. (You will need to turn right toward a stone wall at the bottom.)

At the riverside, turn right to follow The Two Rivers Way under a road bridge and look for the footbridge over the Chew to the car park on your left.

12: MANNING'S WOOD

OR 'THE SACRIFICIAL RAM' 7.5M

From the Shield and Dagger, East Dundry Road, Whitchurch

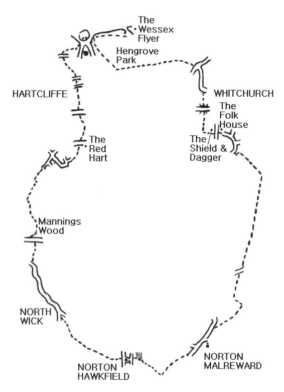

The heavy horns on this ram's head will do him little good if the regional planners have their way. The roundabout that decorates his head is the lynch pin of the ring road extension, designed to join the A4, the A37 and the A38. The idea is that the road will sweep around Whitchurch across the footpath between the Folk House and Norton Malreward and then crash into the edge of Hartcliffe along the line of the path from the Red Hart to the roundabout.

Every year, a group of people from Bedminster and Southville make the trek up the hill to source of the Malago River in Manning's Wood, where they have a picnic. The Malago is a muddy stream, which runs into the New Cut of the River Avon through a culvert, but it is river with a history cherished by those whose families have lived in the Bedminster area for generations. If the regional planners have their way it looks as though that will be having their picnic by the side of a dual carriageway.

This route makes a link between the Malago Source and Whitchurch and also links the two to the Maiden Head stream on the other side of the ridge, which runs through North Wick and Norton Malreward.

I have started the route description from the Shield and Dagger, which I found when I was developing the Maes Knoll route, but it would be equally possible to start from the Wessex Flyer in the Hengrove Leisure park or at the Red Hart on the corner of Barbour Road and Bishport Avenue at both of which, refreshments are available. The 20, 21, 50 and 51 buses all stop near the Shield and Dagger. The 36, 75, 76, and 77 all pass the Red Hart, and the 52, 90 and 636 stop near the Hengrove Leisure Centre.

FROM THE SHIELD AND DAGGER TO MANNING'S WOOD

From the pub, turn right again onto a footpath into a green open space.

Turn right again past a children's playground toward Whitchurch Lane, which is crossed by an underpass as well as the usual footpaths.

Follow the footpath ahead into Briery Leaze Road and follow it through a green open space to Bamfield Road.

Cross the road into Hengrove Park Recreation Ground.

Go straight ahead across a track and bear left toward the left hand edge of a copse in the distance.

Pick up the track in the rough grass past the copse and follow up onto the bank that surrounds the recreation ground.

The bank encircles a low-lying boggy area.

Just before a branch off the path goes straight ahead, look for a path that descends through the brambles on the left toward Hengrove Way.

Over a barrier, turn left along the pavement towards a tunnel under Whitchurch Lane.

When you emerge into the open roundabout, turn left to find the subway under Hartcliffe Way.

On the other side, turn right alongside another section of Hengrove Way, until you can turn left across another road, which is a branch off Whitchurch Lane, to a gate onto a path beside the Malago Stream.

Follow the stream uphill over two roads until you reach a footbridge on the left.

Cross the bridge and continue on the other bank until you can cross back over a stone footbridge.

Follow the right bank to Hareclive Road and continue on that bank up to Bishport Avenue.

Cross over and follow the path through a litter strew path until it leads into Macey's Road.

Keep left until you can take the third turning on the right down Englishcombe Road.

At the end, turn left uphill past the end of Mellent Avenue until you reach a gate into a field.

(When I was there last there were a pair of stiles over a pipeline of some sort)

Climb a steep path involving some twists and some steps into an enclosed track.

When you can, turn left into the open space known as Manning's Wood.

Turn right up the hill and follow the path to the source of the Malago Stream, which has been developed into something of a feature.

FROM THE SOURCE TO NORTON MALREWARD

Past the spring, keep as close as practicable to the hedge on the right until you exit over a stile onto a farm track.

Turn right and go past the barrier onto a road.

Turn left and look for a stile on the right.

Go straight down the field between the crop rows to a track along the bottom of the field.

Turn right and go round the hedge corner to exit onto the road by a stile beside the gate. (Use the gate if the stile is still overgrown!)

Turn left and descend the road until you reach a road junction.

Turn right then immediately left over a stile into a field.

Go straight ahead across the field to another stile. (NB The last time I followed this route, the farmer had confined the path to the edge with an electric sheep fence in this and the following two fields.)

Over this stile follow the well-used path to an unnecessarily substantial double stile and bridge over a rivulet.

From the bridge take the first stile on the left and carry on across the next field to a double stile and bridge.

Turn immediately left over another stile.

Keep going parallel to the left hand hedge a substantial footbridge with astile at either end.

Keep going through the scrub to find a stile into the field on the left

Over this stile, bear right to find a stile into a road in Norton Hawkfield.

I have never seen a hawk here, but I have seen a raven, which also flies over the fields to the north of Chew Magna.

In the road, turn right and then first left. (Or left and immediately right - it comes to the same thing!)

At the junction turn left then right through a gate into a farmyard.

Go straight on through the farmyard until you must bear right onto a farm track.

Go through two gates to follow the edge of a mini-escarpment around a wire fence.

Go through one kissing gate and bear right along a line of three horse chestnut trees to another.

Bear right along the wire fence to yet another kissing gate onto the road.

Turn left through the village past the church, and then look for a stile on the right, as the road bends to the left.

In the field, the official footpath goes diagonally across the arable field, but there is an obviously preferable track around the right hand edge of the field to the double stile over a bridge in the diagonally opposite corner. (The first stile was destroyed the last time I was there.)

Over the stile, go slightly left of straight ahead to another stile to the left of a tree*, and continue on same the line to a kissing gate onto a minor road.

*A section of the Wansdyke is shown on the map just before this stile. The only visible sign is a line of slightly raised ground running roughly parallel to the hedge. It does not look like a Dark Age fortification, but it could have looked more convincing before it was ploughed out.

In the road, go through the kissing gate opposite.

In the field, head for the kissing gate in the distant hedge below Whitewood Farm.

Through this gate and the bridge a gate which follow it, go straight ahead to another kissing gate.

Keep going alongside a narrow field on the right, which follows the course of a disused railway.

Through the next kissing gate, you need to head for a kissing gate in the diagonally opposite corner of the field. In 2006, this route was obstructed by the construction of a pipeline. It was then necessary to follow the right hand hedge over a pair of stiles on either side of the fenced construction site before heading for the kissing gate.

In the next field, follow the left hand hedge to find another kissing gate into a path through some houses into Emmett Wood (a close).

At the end of the close, turn right into another road and follow it round a bend to a bus stop.

Go straight ahead into Half Acre Close and follow the path at the end past Bridge Farm Junior School into East Dundry Lane opposite the Shield and Dagger Pub.

13: DUNDRY SLOPES
OR 'CHICKEN' 8M
From the Dundry Inn, Dundry

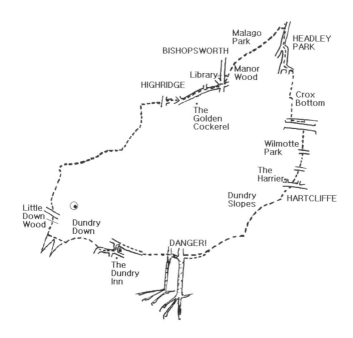

This bird reflects the state of mind of some people who live beyond the boundary of the city. I have led many groups of runners along versions of this route, which goes in towards the centre rather than out from it, before ever I heard of the Community Forest Path, and I have been surprised at the attitude of some of them at the prospect of leaving the countryside to enter into the Hartcliffe estate.
I have some sympathy. In TACH, we run by torchlight in the winter, and one of most atmospheric runs I can remember took place one foggy January night. As we ran down through Willmotte Park in Hartcliffe, there were fires all around from

people burning rubbish under cover of darkness. The fog made it seem like a scene from Mordor, but what they made of us, running off the hill in our head-torches, I have no idea!

There is evidence of some mutual suspicion all along the boundary of the city.

However, this route is well worth persevering with. The views across the city are magnificent under nearly all atmospheric conditions, and it is a green route throughout, except for some short stretches of road in Highridge, Bishopsworth and Headley Park.

It is possible to park in Dundry at the car park next to Dundry Down, or at the Dundry Inn with the landlord's permission. The 672 and 674 buses do visit Dundry, but it is not a frequent service, so if I was using public transport, I would get the 75, 76 or 77 and start from Bishopsworth Library. That way, you could get a drink half way round with a clear conscience.

FROM THE DUNDRY INN TO BISHOPSWORTH LIBRARY

From the Dundry Inn, turn left and then right around the Church and then first right into the lane along the edge of the escarpment to a gate by a turning circle. There is a stile beside the gate, but it is generally overgrown with nettles, so most people climb over the gate.

Continue to another stile by a gate into a field beside a farm. Go straight ahead along a gully to a stile into the field ahead. Keep going straight ahead down a track. The right of way is supposed to go through the wire fence into a scrubby patch but that was impossible the last time I was there. Instead, turn right through one gate and then left to another, which leads onto a metalled road.

Go straight ahead to the junction with the Bristol Road.

Cross the road into a lane and follow it through a gate near a house on the right (which is usually open) until you reach a gate into a field.

Go over the stile next to the gate and follow the hedge on your left to a stile by another gate.

Over this stile keep going along the hedge on your left to a stile hidden in the corner of the field. Do not climb the stile, which is made of tubular steel. Instead turn left through a gap and follow the right hand hedge through a gap in a wire fence beside an old redundant stile to the corner of the field.

There is a squeeze through the wire fence to the tubular steel stile into the Dundry Slopes. However, the path down to Bishport Avenue is overgrown with brambles, so it is best to turn left immediately into the next field over a post and rail fence, and continue down hill in that field until you come across a gap into the thicket on the right.

Follow the narrow muddy path down between the brambles until the area opens up near the backs of some houses.

Bear left down to a kissing gate onto Bishport Avenue.

Cross the road, turn right and then, after crossing one road, turn left into a green space between the houses, called Wilmotte Park.

Keep going through the park over three roads to emerge under a dual carriageway.

On far side of the flyover, turn left and continue until you see a footpath on the right into a green open space.

Follow the path downhill downhill, past two paths up to the left and one across a bridge over the stream to the right. Take the third metalled path on the left and follow it onto a grassy knoll with a kissing gate at the far end.

Through the kissing gate, follow the path past a horse field on the right to emerge through another kissing gate onto a road. In the road turn right and then right again.

Keep on the right hand pavement down the hill until you come to an ivy covered lamppost.

Cross the road and go through a hole in the hedge into Malago Park.

Go straight ahead, diagonally across the old course of the Malago River to a metalled footpath.

Follow the path upstream for about a kilometre until you emerge onto a road opposite some shops.

(There is an alternative route that runs on the left hand side of the stream, if you prefer a bit of a scramble through the trees of Manor Wood. I have left it out on this occasion, because this route is hard enough as it is! In any case, I have described that route in the Two Brooks route, which follows this one.)

On the road, turn right up to pedestrian crossing by Bishopsworth Library.

FROM BISHOPSWORTH LIBRARY TO THE DUNDRY INN

Over the crossing, turn left, cross King's Head Road and turn right up Vicarage Road.

Turn right up Spartley Drive, opposite some shops and the Golden Cockerel public house.

Take the footpath on the left between some houses to emerge in Geoffrey Close.

Go straight on to a T-junction and turn left, then right up the Elsbert Drive towards the fields.

Over a stile into the field, go straight on keeping a fence on your left.

Over another stile (protected by a pallet) keep straight on to a stile in the corner of the field.

Over this stile, bear left to a metal stile (often obscured by vegetation).

Over this stile, go straight ahead alongside the hedge on your left to a stile in the corner.

Over this stile, bear diagonally right across the field to a stile in a wire fence on the other side of a patch of ground that gets very muddy in wet weather.

Over the stile, turn right and follow the right hand hedge through the remains of a wire fence (Caution!) to a gate about fifty metres from right hand corner of the field.

Over the gate (marked with a Community Forest sticker), go diagonally left to the bottom left hand corner of the field, where there is a stile and a bridge over a stream at the bottom of a slippery path concealed by brambles.

Over the bridge, follow the fenced path until you reach a bridge and a stile into a field.

In field, follow right hand hedge up to gate. There is stile to the left of the gate, but that was impassable the last time I was there.

Through the gate, go straight across the field to a stile in the far hedge onto a track.

Turn left and go up hill to a stile.

Over the stile follow the path across the field to a wooden bridge.

Over the bridge, turn right and follow the path uphill, with a hedge on your right until the path branches right through a gap in the hedge.

Through the gap, turn left and continue on uphill, with the hedge on your left, to emerge onto a road.

Go left then right up a muddy track to a gate.

Through the gate, look for a path uphill towards the radio masts on the left.

Climb the stone stile next to the mast and follow the metalled track across Dundry Down toward the Church.

The public car park is just through the gate onto the road.

The pub is past the car park next to the church.

14: TWO BROOKS
OR 'THE REDBREASTED KOOKABURRA'
(7 or 8M approx)
From the Coronation, Dean Lane, Southville

It ought to be a Robin, of course, because Ashton Gate is the home of Bristol City Football Club; but it obviously isn't one of those! It looks much more like the Australian bird, although its beak looks a little stunted.

This route mirrors the first, in that it had its origins in a pub - in this instance the Coronation in Dean Lane. And like that route 'out from the centre' it begins in the inner city and ends up in the countryside. However, in this case, the countryside is no simulacrum preserved by the Victorians, like the Downs, but the real thing, complete with mud and water in the winter. The two routes meet briefly on the railway bridge across the New Cut onto Spike Island, thus completing the circle around Bristol. Manor Wood is the preserve of the Malago Valley Conservation Group, which serves Bedminster Down, Bishopsworth, Hartcliffe, Headley Park, Highridge and Withywood (BS13 more or less). It shares with 'Sustainable Southville', based at the Southville Centre, an interest in the annual trek from the car park at Asda in Bedminster to the Malago Source on the Dundry Ridge. We have adapted the route of the trek to turn it into a circular route linked to the Forest Path, starting from the Coronation in Dean Lane, a choice determined by the quality of the beer!

FROM THE CORONATION TO BISHOPSWORTH

From the pub, turn left towards the New Cut of the River Avon.

Take the second tuning on the right up Southville Road past St Paul's Church.

At the end of Lucky Lane, turn right and then cross over St John's Road into the Asda car park.

Carry on through the car park, past the supermarket to emerge in Bedminster Parade.

Cross over by the pedestrian crossing and then turn right and then left into Philip Street.

The trek takes a slightly different route at this point, but 'The Apple Tree', a rough cider house on the left and the Windmill Hill City Farm on the right make this a more interesting approach to the Greenway.

At the end of the road, cross over Whitehouse Lane and go through the tunnel under the railway ahead.

Through the tunnel, turn right onto the cycle path, which runs alongside the railway at the bottom of Victoria Park.

When the cycle path emerges into a road, turn right to cross a road emerging from under the railway to find the next section of the cycle path.

This is where the Malago trek joins the Greenway. The trekkers have followed the underground path of the Malago more closely than we have, as is shown by the sight of the stream disappearing under the railway on the right.

When the path emerges into a small industrial estate, follow the stream to St John's Lane, which is a lot busier than it sounds!

Cross the road by the pedestrian crossing and go straight ahead to cross another road into a footpath on the right hand side of the stream (the cycle path is on the other side at this point.)

At the next road, turn right and then left along the next stretch of the Greenway.

It is not possible to follow the Malago through the industrial estate on the far side of the next road, so you need to turn right and then left down Hastings Road to Hartcliffe Way.

Turn left to a very necessary pedestrian crossing and then left to find Vale Lane on your right.

This road through another industrial estate belies its name, but past the warehouses, you will find the entrance to the Malago Greenway Park on your right.

The Malago is culverted at this point, but you can just make out some water in a cage near the park entrance. It must have been a dangerous beast once to need such treatment!

Follow the old stream bed, indicated by a broad gully in the grass.

At the end bear left into Manor Wood.

The trekkers keep to the tarmac path at this point, but they have the delights of Mannings Wood to look forward to and a picnic on Dundry Ridge. The going is quite treacherous through the wood, especially in wet weather, so you may prefer to follow the trekkers at this point.

Follow the path through the wood. For most of its length the path keeps high above the Malago stream. (I would avoid the first set of steep steps down to the right. The upper path is preferable, in spite of some fallen branches.)

When the path comes down to the streamside beside a scorched tree, cross over the stream by means on some stepping stones and turn left towards the exit from the park. (If the stream is high and you do not wish to get your feet wet, it is simple enough to keep straight ahead and cross by means of a bridge.) When you leave the park, turn right up to the pedestrian crossing next to Bishopsworth Library.

FROM THE LIBRARY TO THE CORONATION

Cross over Bishopsworth Road on the zebra crossing and then turn left across King's Head Lane.

Turn right up Vicarage Road past the manor house.

Carry on uphill until you reach Spartley Drive on your right. (The Golden Bottle is over the grass on the left if you are in need of refreshment.)

About thirty metres up Spartley Drive, look for a path between the house on the left.

This path leads through into Geoffrey Close, which leads up to Highridge Green. A diagonal path across the verge indicates the way to Elsbert Drive opposite.

Do not follow the road to the right but carry straight on past some impressive gates to a stile into the fields.

From here there is a choice of routes to Colliter's Brook.

SHORT CUT

Turn right over the stile near Highridge Farm and follow a sequence of four stiles along the backs of the houses until you debouch onto the side of the A38.

Cross the road with care and follow the drive to Yewtree farm opposite until it bends to the right.

Go straight ahead over a stile and continue straight on along the hedge on your left, past a stile in the hedge and down a steep slope to a stile into a thicket.

FOR THE LONGER ROUTE

Over the stile, go straight on keeping a fence on your left.

Over another stile (protected by a pallet) keep straight on to a stile in the corner of the field.

Over this stile, bear left to a metal stile (often obscured by vegetation).

Over stile, go straight ahead alongside the hedge on your left to a stile in the corner.

Over this stile, bear diagonally right across the field to a stile in a wire fence on other side of a patch of ground that gets very muddy in wet weather.

Over the stile, turn right and follow the right hand hedge through the remains of a wire fence (Caution!) to the right hand corner of the field.

Turn right through the gap in the hedge closest to the corner. Through the gap, bear left to a stile in the corner of the next field.

Over this stile, bear right to find a stile beside a gate onto a track down to the A38.

Over the main road go right to find a stile.

Over this stile, go straight across the field to another stile.

Over this stile, bear right to find a stile along the hedge on your right.

Over this stile, follow the hedge on your right to a pair of stiles over a farm track, then carry on down-slope in the same direction to another pair of stiles over the access road to the landfill site.

Bear left to a stile in a wire fence and carry on, on same line, to another stile in a hedge.

Over this stile, turn sharp left down the hedge side and over another stile into a thicket.

This is where the two routes join.

Track right through the thicket to find a stile out into a field.

Track left around the brambles to find a path to a double stile and bridge over Colliter's Brook.

Turn right in between the stream and the landfill site (ignoring a second bridge on your right) to find a tunnel under the main line to the Exeter and beyond.

In the open follow the right hand edge of the field past factories and deep water until the path goes through a gap in the hedge ahead.

Keep straight on alongside the Ashton diversion channel. *This carries the water of Colliter's Brook to Longmoor Brook, whose waters are captured in a tunnel in the Longbrook Trading Estate, to debouch into the River Avon downstream of the Weston road bridge.*

Either:

Turn right through the first gate on your right across the channel and then left to another bridge, turn right to follow the right hand hedge around the field until you reach a gap onto a bridge leading to Ashton Vale. *This is not a right of way, but it does enable you to use a section of a right of way that is otherwise blocked.* Or:

Keep straight on until the next gate and bridge on your right. In the field, follow the left hand edge around to the same gap and bridge (which will be on your left.) *This is a right of way and it follows Longmoor Brook, but it spoils the artistic impression of the map!*

In either case, turn left on the path alongside the remains of Colliter's Brook. (Take care crossing the railway line, which is still active.)

In Winterstoke Road, cross the traffic beside the roundabout and then turn left and then right down Marsh Road.

As the road bends to the right, go straight on into Greville Smyth Park and head for the old bonded warehouse opposite. Leave the park opposite the warehouse and cross the road carefully to enter the open space to the left of the warehouse. *There is a vegetarian café at the Riverside Garden Centre, which can be reached down the right hand side of the warehouse.*

Bear left through the trees to Ashton Railway Bridge over the Avon.

This area has attracted the attention of The Ashton Junction Wildlife Partnership (AJWP). This represents five special interest groups co-ordinated by the Create Centre, whose building provides a focal point for the area.

Turn right along the path beside the New Cut - *looked after by FrANC (Friends of the Avon New Cut).*

Follow the path until it emerges onto the pavement beside Cumberland Road.

Turn right on the footbridge to Coronation Road and then turn right and then left into Dean Lane to return to the pub.

15: THE MERCHANTS' OR THE DRAGON (6M)

From the Merchants' Arms in Merchants Road, Hotwells

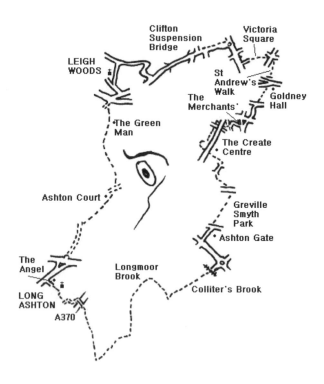

This dragon's head poking across the boundary of the city and county of Bristol into North Somerset could represent that most controversial aspect of Bristol's history: the activities of its merchants. Their involvement in the slave trade means that the expression 'Merchants' Quarter' is now thought to be too controversial to name the redevelopment of Bristol's shopping centre. The Merchants Arms public house, where this route starts, has no connections with the slave trade as far as I know. However, the same could not be said of Ashton Court, which was built by

the Smyth family, who were also connected with Greville Smyth Park. They made most of their money from coal mining, but they also made money from trade in the West Indies, which inevitably meant that they were involved in the slave trade. Also implicated in the slave trade was Thomas Goldney, whose family built Goldney Hall, according to the National Archives Website.

Whether any of this has any relevance nowadays is another question. Apologies are often asked for. But what is the point of apologising for the activities of the dead? However, it is true to say that the Society of Merchant Venturers of Bristol, the body that regulated the slave trade in Bristol, is still in existence and manages charitable trusts that run two private schools and some old peoples' homes. It will soon also manage a comprehensive school in Withywood. The Society also shares the management of the Downs with Bristol City Council and may have some members in common with the mysterious charitable trust that manages the Clifton Suspension Bridge The bridge owes its existence to the bequest of Bristol merchant William Vick, a vintner.

The number 500 Harbour Link bus stops in Merchants' Road opposite the Merchants' Arms. There is no parking in Merchants' Road, but there is a small car park in Charles Place behind the pub.

Refreshments are available en route at the Angel in Long Ashton and in the café behind Ashton Court. There are also plenty of pubs and cafés in Clifton, several of which are visible from the route. The Merchant's Arms itself is a tiny Bath Ale's boozer with plenty of character. However, there are several other good pubs in the area and you would certainly need a bus or a taxi home if you tried them all!

FROM MERCHANT STREET TO THE COUNTY BOUNDARY

Go down Charles Place, the back lane beside the Merchants' Arms.

Follow the lane around the corner to a junction.

Make your way under the flyover to the dockside. (Take care crossing the roads on the way, especially the last, which leads onto the Portway. Also, be aware that once you have passed the gate, there is nothing to stop you falling in the dock!)

Cross over the top of the lock-gate and a wooden bridge.

When you emerge on a slip road, turn right on the path alongside the river. *(This is the point of Spike Island, which separates the New Cut from the Floating Harbour.)*

This path takes you back under the flyover and emerges by the Create Centre. *(Note the Longmoor Brook outflow on the right before the bridge.)*

Go past the gate and make your way to the old railway bridge over the New Cut.

On the far side, bear left across the grass to emerge on the road beside another red-brick warehouse opposite Greville Smyth Park.

Bear right across the park to come out onto the road opposite Ashton Gate (Bristol City FC's ground).

Turn right and then left down Marsh Road to Winterstoke Road. Turn left to the roundabout and cross the road to Baron's Close a cul-de-sac between the warehouses.

Cross the railway line at the end. Take care. It is not much used, but it is by means abandoned.

Follow the path alongside Colliter's Brook until it is possible to turn right beside a bridge into the fields.

Go straight across the first field to Longmoor Brook on the far side.

Turn left alongside the brook a carry on until you reach a concrete bridge.

Turn left alongside a ditch. *(It is actually a channel designed to divert water from Colliter's Brook into the Longmoor Brook, which discharges into the River Avon through a tunnel opposite the end of Spike Island. The channel marks the boundary between the City and County of Bristol and North Somerset.)*

Climb the stile beside a new copse in the corner of the field. Turn right after a gap in a hedge, which brings you back onto the Community Forest Path.

FROM THE COUNTY BOUNDARY TO THE SUSPENSION BRIDGE

Follow the hedge on the right past one gate to a second.

Through the gate, turn right and follow a grassy track around the edge of a linear wood and look for a gate on the right that functions as a stile.

Bear right across the field to a gated bridge over the Ashton Brook *(called Longmoor Brook further downstream).*

Go straight ahead to a cattle bridge over the Long Ashton By-pass.

Follow the cattle track (often deep in slurry) around a bend to the right and another to the left, after which there is a horse gate on the right beside the graveyard wall

Go straight ahead and look for a kissing gate into the churchyard on your right.

Turn left past the church to emerge in Church Lane, which joins the main road through Long Ashton beside the **Angel Inn**.

Turn right and follow the road toward the gateway into the Ashton Court Estate.

Take great care crossing the main road and follow the drive toward the house.

Turn right past a pair of black iron gates into an ornamental wood and follow the track past an ice-house to another pair of iron gates into the garden.

The path through the garden goes up some steps and through some trees to emerge at the back of Ashton Court (where there is a café and a visitor centre.)

Bear left across the grass and between the parked cars to more grass and a track against a deer fence.

Turn left and follow the track between the fence and the wood to a kissing gate.

Once past the gate, look for a path through the deer park on the right, marked by white posts.

This takes you past the corner of a wood and the statue of a green man's head featured on the cover of this book to another kissing gate.

Carry on to the main gateway out of the estate and use the pedestrian crossing to cross Rownham Hill and Bridge Road. Turn right toward the Suspension Bridge, but turn left up Church Road and then right up Vicarage Road to emerge in North Road near the University Botanical Gardens.

Turn right alongside Nightingale Valley to emerge back on Bridge Road near the Suspension Bridge.

FROM THE SUSPENSION BRIDGE TO MERCHANTS' ROAD

Cross the Suspension Bridge and follow Suspension Bridge Road to a min-roundabout.

Turn right and continue along Clifton Down Road to a zebra crossing.

Cross over and go down Boyce's Avenue, past the Arcade on your left and the Albion on your right through the arch into Victoria Square.

Follow the diagonal path across the square and cross the main road into a car park, on the other side of which is St Andrew's Walk, all that remains of St Andrew's Church, which was destroyed during the blitz.

At the other end of the Walk cross one road and go down the path across the grass to another. Cross this road to the corner of Goldney Avenue.

Go straight on to Goldney Lane past Goldney Hall, which is indicated by a sign to the Lion.

Keep going downhill through Goldney Lane (Mind the Steps!) and Ambra Vale to emerge on Hotwells Road.

Turn right and then left to return to Merchants' Road and the Merchants' Arms.